The Cyrus Anointing

Accessing Treasures of Darkness and Hidden Riches of Secret Places

Publisher: Shofar Media House

For enquiries and speaking invitations, please inbox our Facebook Page below;

www.facebook.com/CyrusInternationalNetworkOfMarketplaceApostles

First Publication 2018

Publication © Ndoda H Phungulwa 2018

All rights reserved. No part of this publication may be reproduced, stored in a retrieval system or transmitted, in any form or by any means, electronic, mechanical, photocopying, recording or otherwise, without the prior written permission of the copyright owner, the author.

PUBLISHER: Shofar Media House

COVER DESIGN: Ntobeko Mjijwa, Fine Art Illustrator, NMU Graduate

ISBN 978 0 620 71772 4 (print)

CONTENTS

Acknowledgments	5
Preface	7
Foreword	10
Introduction	13
The Mission of Cyrus	18
Cyrus: the Shepherd of the LORD	31
Cyrus: the Man of Righteousness	41
Cyrus: the Ravenous Bird	51
Cyrus: the Anointed	61
Cyrus: Strengthened By God	80
Subduing Nations	90
Stripping the Armour of Kings	96
Treasures of Darkness & Hidden Riches of Secret Places	106
Cyrus: God's Battle Axe and Weapons of War	121
Resident Authority in the Cyrus Anointing	129
The Army Marshalled By Cyrus	141

Cyrus: The Prophetic Shadow of Jesus Christ	155
Gearing for a Hostile Takeover	171
Exposing Modern Day Babylon	181
The Fall of Babylon	199

Acknowledgements

Above all else, I want to thank my heavenly Father for the privilege, grace and honour of being entrusted with such an undeserved understanding of His mysteries and revelation. This book is my sincere heartfelt offering to the Almighty God. May it give God all the praise, glory and honour He deserves by making a significant contribution towards uplifting and shaping the Church into being the Mountain of the House of the LORD prophesied in both Isaiah chapter 2 and Micah chapter 4. I also want to thank God for sustaining and keeping me sane through some of the most trying and difficult times that I have been through.

Secondly, I want to thank my family (parents and siblings) for their unwavering belief in me and all that God has called and destined for me to be. I also want to thank my family for their support at all times. I am blessed to have you as my family and I would never in a trillion years trade you for anything or anyone else. I love you all a lot more than you can ever imagine. You have remained true, loving, steadfast and unwavering in your love and support for me when there was no one else that I could lean on. For that, I am forever indebted to you all. I LOVE YOU ALL.

"For we know in part, and we prophesy in part"

(1 Corinthians 13:9 KJV)

Preface

God is a God that is forever speaking. He is constantly on a mission to renew, empower and equip His Church. This continual renewal, empowering and equipping of the Church is not only necessary but fundamental for the Church of Jesus Christ to remain relevant and also to make a tangible impact in the world we live in today. This continual renewal, empowering and equipping of the Church matures and prepares the Church of Jesus Christ for all that which God has in store for the Church.

One of the key reasons why it is necessary and fundamental for the Church of Jesus Christ to experience continual renewal, empowering and equipping from God is because, the Church of Jesus Christ is a living organism. The Church is dynamic and cannot afford to remain static. That which is static and stagnant dies. It ceases to live. A Church that is a representative of the only true and living God cannot cease to live.

It is against this reason that God is currently in the process of releasing the Cyrus Anointing and raising men, women and children to walk in the same grace and anointing that God Almighty placed upon King Cyrus of the Medo-Persian Empire. I am not in any way suggesting that the Cyrus Anointing is the be all and end all. I am simply advocating that the Cyrus Anointing is one of the key tools, instruments and weapons that God uses as part of His military artillery.

Now, many might be cautious when it comes to embracing the Cyrus Anointing. I would expect no less from any Bible believing and Jesus Christ confessing child of God. The caution though, should not in any way cause us to shrink away from receiving all that which God has in store for us because of fear. The approach of any true believer in Jesus Christ should be the same as that of the Berean Church in the book of Acts. The Bible says; *"These were more noble than those in Thessalonica, in that they received the word with all readiness of mind, and searched the scriptures daily, whether those things were so." **(Acts 17:11)**.*

In Isaiah 45, we find that though King Cyrus was a gentile king, he was anointed by God. It is a well-known truth that under the Old Testament, only Israel's priests, prophets, kings and judges were anointed by God. King Cyrus was an exception to the rule. It is critical to remember that the Bible speaks to us in types, shadows, allegories and similitudes.

It is for that reason that the release of the Cyrus Anointing in the present day is based on the law of double reference. Edwin Hartell defines the law of double reference as follows; "…te peculiarity of the writings of the Holy Spirit, by which a passage applying primarily to a person or event near at hand is used by Him at a later time as applying to the person of Christ, or the affairs of His kingdom." It is for that reason that this book is more about looking into the prophetic parallels between the mission and assignment of King Cyrus of the Medo-Persian Empire against ancient Babylon and the mission and assignment of those called and anointed with the Cyrus Anointing today.

It is my intention through this book to pull back the veil from the eyes of the Church of Jesus Christ by sharing the nuggets of truth and revelation that God has placed in my heart over a lengthy period of time. This was as early as August 2000, when God by the Holy Spirit began to open my eyes and warm my heart to the truth of the Cyrus Anointing and the Fall of Babylon. It is my sincere hope and desire that this book will contribute significantly to the shaping of the Church of Jesus Christ and spur the saints of God towards the fulfilment of their God ordained destinies by capturing the entire marketplace and bring it under the Lordship and Rule of Jesus Christ the King of kings and Lord of Glory.

Foreword

Ndoda Phungulwa has written on a subject which may be perceived as controversial within conventional Christianity. What he terms a Cyrus Anointing is a demonstration of the providence of God using a heathen king to fulfil the divine purposes of God concerning his people Israel. Although this Cyrus was a heathen king, God chose him to do a great work for him. God still chooses his Cyruses in our modern day who ought to be aware of the fact that God does not change. He is the same yesterday, today and forever. The latter is the premise on which Phungulwa writes. The same God who used Cyrus in those ancient times is still able to use a category of people who fall within the Cyrus classification. In one sense they can be kings like Cyrus or represent principles of a king like political leaders or legislators. They may also be occupying any position or office of significance in any field of influence be it in business, government, education etc.

The unique attribute about these 'Cyrus like' people is that they possess a favour that makes them stand out from the rest. Cyrus although he was a king and therefore possessing power and influence there was an extra benefit he enjoyed and that was the favour of God upon his life. Whatever he touched, God made it to succeed because God had chosen him. The favour of God over Cyrus made him look like a saint. God endorsed his steps as righteous. Cyrus type of people are like shepherds who guard, feed and protect God's people in fulfilling the plan of God for their lives. These people do not live for themselves but they live for the greater good of others. The kindness that Cyrus showed to the children of Israel made him a true shepherd and also a protector of God's people.

The Cyrus type of people protect those who are vulnerable especially economically. God gives them wealth and financial favour to protect the poor from falling prey to the worldly system which Phungulwa calls the Babylonian system. These Cyrus type of people operate in an ability that is unique to heroes. This ability is what Phungulwa refers to as the Cyrus Anointing. This is the anointing that is typical to heroes like Cyrus hence it is called the Cyrus Anointing.

The Cyrus kind of people are not self centered or selfish but they live for something bigger than themselves. They live to fulfil their God given mandate. They are very focused on their assignment and will fight anything that tends to resist them in their mission. They have a high level of faith and persistence to fight anything that is opposed to the plan of God for His people. God uses these type of people to humble all the proud and to lift up the humbled hence they become 'God's battle axe'.

There's therefore a need to train the people of God to understand themselves as arrows that God is calling out and sending them to the world to take over the systems of the earth (the Babylonian systems) and bring the rule of Christ using a Cyrus Anointing which is nothing but a type and shadow of the anointing upon Christ as seen in Isaiah 61:1-7 and referenced by Christ in Luke 4:18.

I recommend this book for those who are serious with the call of destroying Babylon and establishing Christ's rule in the earth.

By Mangaliso M Matshobane
Founder of Community Church and Apostolic leader of ACT(a network of churches called Apostolic Churches Together)

Introduction

It was during the reign of King Hezekiah that Isaiah prophesied that the nation of Israel would end up exiled and enslaved in Babylon. When King Hezekiah fell sick, God told Isaiah to prophesy that Hezekiah should set his house in order as he would not recover but die.

On hearing this prophetic word, Hezekiah turned to the wall and cried to God. Before Isaiah left the courts of the palace of the king, God told him to go back and tell Hezekiah that God was granting him a fifteen year life extension.

On receipt of the news of Hezekiah's recovery, the king of Babylon (an insignificant little kingdom at the time) sent envoys and messengers with gifts to celebrate the recovery, healing and restoration of King Hezekiah.

It was at this occasion that King Hezekiah exposed Israel to a potential enemy when he showed the Babylonians everything that was in his kingdom. In his boasting, King Hezekiah showed the Babylonians all the treasures, arsenal and energy sources of his kingdom.

It was at this time that Prophet Isaiah showed up and asked him three questions; "What said these men? And from whence came they unto thee?.....What have they seen in thine house?" (Isaiah 39:3-4). It was at this point that Isaiah gave the following prophecy;

"Hear the word of the LORD of hosts: Behold, the days come, that all that is in thine house, and that which thy fathers have

laid up in store until this day, shall be carried to Babylon: nothing shall be left, saith the LORD. And of thy sons that shall issue from thee, which thou shalt beget, shall they take away; and they shall be eunuchs in the palace of the king of Babylon. Then Hezekiah said to Isaiah, Good is the word of the LORD which thou hast spoken. He said moreover, For there shall be peace and truth in my days." **(Isaiah 39:5-8)**

The fulfilment of the above prophecy takes place during the reign of three kings, namely; Jehoiakim, Jehoiachin and Zedekiah. There are several passages of scripture that chronicle the fall of Jerusalem including; 2 Kings 24 & 25, Jeremiah 39 & 52 and Daniel 1. The result, as prophesied by Isaiah, children (Daniel, Hananiah, Mishael and Azariah) of royal descent ended up eunuchs in Babylon.

Israel was in this state of complete defeat, hopelessness and helplessness. The author assumes that the reader is well versed on this background and state of the nation of Israel. The reader will get a detailed, structured, comprehensive understanding of *The Cyrus Anointing* as the author's chapter outline is as follows;

Chapter one of the book introduces the reader to *The Mission of Cyrus*. The author outlines the biblical and historic mission of King Cyrus and also outlines mission of the Modern Day Cyrus Anointing.

Chapter two of the book looks into *Cyrus: the Shepherd of the LORD*. The author unpacks the role and function of a shepherd and also outlines the kind of heart and attitude that is a prerequisite for those that will walk in the fullness of *The Cyrus Anointing*.

Chapter three delves deep into *Cyrus: The Man of Righteousness*. In this chapter the author contends that King Cyrus was a righteous man and also provides scriptural evidence to that effect. He also outlines that righteousness is a prerequisite for those that are keen on tapping into the fullness of *The Cyrus Anointing*.

Chapter four looks into *Cyrus: the Ravenous Bird*. In doing this, the author unpacks the kind of abilities and grace that is resident within *The Cyrus Anointing*.

Chapter five takes a closer look at *Cyrus: the Anointed*. It also looks at what it means to be anointed. The author also takes a deeper look on the type of anointing that *The Cyrus Anointing* being released today really is.

Chapter six looks at *Cyrus: Strengthened By God*. The author looks at how King Cyrus operated in the strength of God and also strengthens the need for those who are called and anointed with *The Cyrus Anointing* today to heavily rely on God's ability.

Chapter seven explains *Subduing Nations*. The author provides revelation and insight into the scope and reach of modern day release of *The Cyrus Anointing*.

Chapter eight *Loosening the Loins of Kings* explains how God weakens all those that are in authority before those that are carrying *The Cyrus Anointing*.

Chapter Nine looks at *Treasures of Darkness and Hidden Riches of Secret Places*. The author provides an insight and understanding of how those called and anointed with *The Cyrus Anointing* can expect to be given and access treasures of darkness and hidden riches of secret places.

Chapter ten looks at *Cyrus: God's Battle Axe and Weapons of War*. The author reveals how those anointed with *The Cyrus Anointing* are to be a tool in God's hand. The chapter also stresses the need to be fully yielded to God.

Chapter eleven looks at the *Resident Authority in the Cyrus Anointing*. The author provides a detailed outline of the authority to make irreversible decrees.

Chapter twelve gives us insight into *The Army Marshalled By Cyrus*. This chapter also emphasises the kind of characteristics that are prerequisite to constitute part of this army. It also emphasizes the importance of teamwork.

Chapter thirteen; *Gearing for a Hostile Takeover* provides a blueprint on how those called and anointed with *The Cyrus Anointing* are to prepare for the assault on Babylon as well as how to position themselves.

Chapter fourteen: *Cyrus: The Prophetic Shadow of Jesus Christ* provides a detailed outline of the prophetic parallels between King Cyrus and Jesus Christ. It also advocates that King Cyrus is a shadow pointing to the reality that is Jesus Christ. The author also shows that those called and anointed with *The Cyrus Anointing* are to do everything to ensure that Jesus Christ is exalted above all.

Chapter Fifteen: *Exposing Modern Day Babylon* looks at the characteristics and traits of ancient Biblical Babylon and also points those out in Modern Day society.

Chapter sixteen: *The Fall of Babylon* provides prophetic insight and revelation into the fall of Modern Day Babylon by contrasting the prophecies about the fall of Babylon against the tragic September 11 terror attacks in the United States of America.

Chapter One

The Mission of Cyrus

When we take a closer look at the life of King Cyrus, it is very evident that there is a clear a conspicuous outline of the mission and assignment that Almighty God gave to King Cyrus. The purpose of this chapter is to look at this mission and assignment that Almighty God gave to King Cyrus. Without exhausting the matter, I want us to take a look at, at least five key pillars that constituted *The Mission of Cyrus*.

The fivefold *Mission of Cyrus* consists of aspects such as; Performing the Pleasure of the LORD, Executing the Counsel of God, Deliverance of Israel, Rebuilding Jerusalem, and Rebuilding the Temple of God. At this point, let us take a closer look at the first aspect or pillar of *The Mission of Cyrus*.

Performing the Pleasure of the LORD

> *"The LORD hath loved him: he will do his pleasure on Babylon, and his arm shall be on the Chaldeans. I, even I, have spoken; yea, I have called him: I have brought him, and he shall make his way prosperous"* **(Isaiah 48:14-15).**

> *"The LORD's chosen ally will carry out his purpose against Babylon; his arm will be against the Babylonians. I, even I, have spoken; yes, I have called him, I will bring him, and he will succeed in his mission"* ***(Isaiah 48:14-15 NIV).***

> *"The LORD has chosen Cyrus as his ally. He will use him to put an end to the empire of Babylon and to destroy the Babylonian armies. I have said it: I am calling Cyrus! I will send him on this errand and will help him succeed"* ***(Isaiah 48:14-15 NLT).***

> *"Did they say that my friend would do what I want done to Babylonia? I was the one who chose him. I have brought him this far, and he will be successful"* ***(Isaiah 48:14-15 CEV).***

One of the things made very clear by the above scripture is that King Cyrus was an ally of God. The English Oxford Dictionaries defines an "ally" as; 1. "A state formally cooperating with another for a military or other purpose", and 2. "A person or organization that cooperates with or helps another in a particular activity". The King James Version of the Bible states that *"The LORD hath loved him"* whilst in the Contemporary English Version, God calls King Cyrus *"my friend"*.

What we see here is that there was a cooperative alliance between heaven and earth. There wasn't a deliverer that could be found from among the Israelites as all their mighty men were held captive in Babylon. Because of that God looked outside of Israel and chose King Cyrus for this honour of being in a league or alliance with God. This means that King Cyrus and his army operated with the strength of the army of heaven whilst they were physically positioned in the earth.

Now, as an ally and friend of God, King Cyrus was entrusted with the mission and assignment of performing the pleasure of the LORD on Babylon. The pleasure of the LORD through King Cyrus was the complete destruction and annihilation of the Babylonian Empire. We are also told in the Bible that the arm of King Cyrus would be upon the Chaldeans or Babylonians.

The arm signifies strength and power. In other words, King Cyrus was empowered and equipped by God Almighty to spoil Babylon and exert the judgment of God upon the nation of Chaldea and the city of Babylon. In fact, Jeremiah, the prophet confirms this as the Bible tells us;

> *"Make bright the arrows; gather the shields: the LORD hath raised up the spirit of the kings of the Medes: <u>for his device is against Babylon, to destroy it</u>; because it is the vengeance of his temple"* ***(Jeremiah 51:11).***

> *"Sharpen the arrows, take up the shields! The LORD has stirred up the kings of the Medes, because <u>his purpose is to destroy Babylon</u>. The LORD will take vengeance, vengeance for his temple"* ***(Jeremiah 51:11 NIV).***

> *"Sharpen the arrows! Lift up the shields! For the LORD has inspired the kings of the Medes to march*

against Babylon and destroy her. This is his vengeance against those who desecrated his Temple" ***(Jeremiah 51:11 NLT).***

"I, the LORD want Babylon destroyed, because its army destroyed my temple. So, you kings of Media, sharpen your arrows and pick up your shields" ***(Jeremiah 51:11 CEV).***

The above scripture quotation also confirms God's irrevocable resolve to destroy Babylon. Jeremiah also tells us that God has stirred up the kings of the Medes. King Cyrus ruled and reigned over the Medo-Persian Empire. The Medo-Persian Empire was a historically very powerful kingdom that conquered and subdued many nations.

God especially chose and anointed King Cyrus to perform this pleasure of destroying Babylon. God also inspired him for this special assignment. There is plenty of scriptural evidence in the Bible that gives us a very clear picture and detailed account of how King Cyrus performed the pleasure of the LORD and destroyed Babylon. To get a clearer understanding of the destruction that King Cyrus brought upon Babylon, please read Isaiah chapters 13, 14, 21, 47 and Jeremiah chapters 50 and 51.

Those that are anointed with the Cyrus Anointing today are also assigned to perform the pleasure of the LORD against Babylon. These are believers that will be assigned specific sectors of the economy to go into such sectors or mountains and dismantle all the works of darkness. They will be assigned into politics, business, education and all the other sectors of the economy.

They will be like Jeremiah who was assigned to; "....root out, and pull down, and to destroy, and to throw down, to build, and to plant" (Jer 1:10). They will root out, pull down, destroy and throw down all the foreign ungodly satanic practices in politics, education, business, entertainment and all other sectors before they build and plant that which is of God.

Executing the Counsel of God

> "Calling a ravenous bird from the east, the man that executeth my counsel from a far country: yea, I have spoken it, I will also bring it to pass; I have purposed it, I will also do it" *(Isaiah 46:11).*

> "From the east I summon a bird of prey; from a far-off land, a man to fulfil my purpose. What I have said, that I will bring about; what I have planned, that I will do" *(Isaiah 46:11 NIV).*

> "I will call a swift bird of prey from the east- a leader from a distant land to come and do my bidding. I have said what I would, and I will do it" *(Isaiah 46:11 NLT).*

> "...and brought someone from a distant land to do what I wanted. He attacked from the east, like a hawk swooping down. Now I will keep my promise and do what I planned" *(Isaiah 46:11 CEV).*

Isaiah lets us in into yet another aspect of *The Mission of Cyrus*. That aspect of *The Cyrus Anointing* is to "execute the counsel of God". The New International Version of the Bible calls it "fulfilling the purpose of God" whilst the New Living Translation of the Bible calls it "doing the bidding of God". The Contemporary English Version of the Bible is much clearer and calls it "doing what God wants done".

Irrespective of which version of the Bible one reads, the prevalent message throughout the different versions of the Bible is that King Cyrus would do that which God wants to be done.

With today's release of the Cyrus Anointing, this aspect of *The Mission of Cyrus* has not changed. Those believers that are anointed with the Cyrus Anointing are also assigned with the duty and responsibility to execute the counsel of God.

This means that it will be very critical for those who desire to walk in and manifest the Cyrus Anointing to develop an intimate relationship with God. This is because, in order for them to execute the counsel of God, they first need to know "what is the specific counsel of God assigned to them?" New Testament believers have the advantage of having the indwelling Holy Spirit. It is Him (Holy Spirit) that will reveal the counsel of God. Remember the Bible teaches us that;

> *"But God hath revealed them unto us by his Spirit: for the Spirit searcheth all things, yea, the deep things of God. For what man knoweth the things of a man, save the spirit of man which is in him? Even so the*

things of God knoweth no man, but the Spirit of God" ***(1 Corinthians 2:10-11).***

There is no substitute for an intimate relationship with God. It is only through this intimate relationship that we will be able to access what is in the mind of God. Those who fail to cultivate this intimate relationship with God will run the risk of "punching the air" without a specific target and a strategy whereas those that have this intimate relationship will have both a target and a strategy. The target is the counsel of God revealed to them by Holy Spirit. They also receive the strategy from Holy Ghost.

Deliverance of Israel

> *"Thus saith the LORD, your redeemer, the holy one of Israel; For your sake I have sent to Babylon, and have brought down all their nobles, and the Chaldeans, whose cry is in the ships"* ***(Isaiah 43:14).***

> *"This is what the LORD says- your Redeemer, the Holy One of Israel: For your sake I will send to Babylon and bring down as fugitives all the Babylonians, in the ships in which they took pride"* ***(Isaiah 43:14 NIV).***

> *"This is what the LORD says- your Redeemer, the Holy One of Israel: "For your sakes I will send an army against Babylon, forcing the Babylonians* to flee in those ships they are so proud of"* ***(Isaiah 43:14 NLT).***

> *"GOD, your Redeemer, The Holy of Israel, says: Just for you, I will march on Babylon. I'll turn the tables on the Babylonians. Instead of whooping it up, they'll be wailing"* ***(Isaiah 43:14 The Message).***

As we can see in the above scripture quotation, God sent King Cyrus and his army to Babylon solely for the sake of Israel. At this time, Israel was exiled in Babylon because of the sins that they had committed against God and because they forsook the only true and living God and worshiped idols. Because of these sins, Israel became vulnerable and God handed them over to the king of Babylon and his army. The Bible makes it clear that King Cyrus was to deliver Israel when it says;

> *"I have raised him up in righteousness, and I will direct all his ways: he shall build my city, <u>and he shall let go my captives</u>, not for price nor reward, saith the LORD of hosts"* ***(Isaiah 45:13).***

> *"I will raise up Cyrus in my righteousness: I will make all his ways straight. He will rebuild my city <u>and set my exiles free</u>, but not for a price or reward, says the LORD Almighty"* ***(Isaiah 45:13 NIV).***

> *"I will raise up Cyrus to fulfil my righteous purpose, and I will guide his actions. He will restore my city <u>and free my captive people</u>- without seeking a reward! I, the LORD of Heaven's Armies, have spoken!"* ***(Isaiah 45:13 NLT).***

> *"And now I've got Cyrus on the move. I've rolled out the red carpet before him. He will build my city. <u>He will bring home my exiles</u>. I didn't hire him to do this. I told him. I, GOD- of- the- Angel- Armies"* ***(Isaiah 45:13 The Message).***

In their time of slavery and exile in Babylon, the Israelites were so defeated and so helpless to an extent that they could not free themselves from their slavery. The level of their brokenness and hopelessness as a people was so severe to an extent that when the king of Babylon conquered them, he left only the poorest sort of people in the land.

The people that were left in Jerusalem were only concerned with survival hence the king of Babylon left them to till the land and send the best produce of the land to Babylon whilst they only lived on the worst of the produce. This was a deliberate strategy by the king of Babylon as he took to slavery and exile all the "cream of the crop" of Israel. It is under these conditions that God had to raise King Cyrus and charge him with the deliverance of Israel.

Even today, those who are called and anointed with the Cyrus Anointing will be charged with the same mandate, mission and assignment of freeing the captive people of God from modern day Babylonian slavery. These are people that are captured by the spirit of the world and live solely according to the standards of the world. The reason for this is because every human being belongs to God.

That is why one of the marks of the Cyrus Anointing today will be heavy involvement with evangelistic campaigns and the winning of souls. Those called and anointed with the Cyrus Anointing will partner very closely with apostles, prophets, evangelists, pastors and teachers that have a heart for soul winning.

To that extent, the modern day release of the Cyrus Anointing will see the carriers of the Cyrus Anointing organizing, funding and hosting massive evangelistic campaigns. It is through these campaigns that many captive in Babylon (the system of the world) will be brought back into the kingdom of God. Through these massive evangelistic campaigns, millions upon millions of souls will be brought under the Lordship of Jesus Christ.

Rebuilding Jerusalem

> *"I have raised him up in righteousness, and I will direct all his ways: he shall build my city, and he shall let go my captives, not for price nor reward, saith the LORD of hosts"* **(Isaiah 45:13).**

> *"That saith of Cyrus, He is my shepherd, and shall perform all my pleasure: even saying to Jerusalem, Thou shalt be built; and to the temple, Thy foundation shall be laid"* **(Isaiah 44:28).**

When the king of Babylon attacked Jerusalem, there was a war that ensued. Naturally that resulted in the destruction of property and the infrastructure of the city of Jerusalem. In fact, the book of Nehemiah gives us a glimpse into the state of the city of Jerusalem. As a matter of fact, Nehemiah took a ride around the city and assessed the damage. Jerusalem had no walls and that made the city vulnerable to attacks from their enemies.

As promised by God through the mouth of Isaiah and Jeremiah, King Cyrus deed indeed rebuild the city of God, Jerusalem. He did this by enacting a decree that cannot be altered, in accordance to the law of the Medes and Persians, which released the Israelites from their slavery and exile in Babylon. He did not end there but he also went further and provided all the financial resources that would be required for the rebuilding of both the city of Jerusalem and the temple of God. For more details on this, kindly refer to 2 Chronicles 36:22-23 and Ezra 1.

Things will not be different with today's release of the Cyrus Anointing. Those believers that are called and anointed with the Cyrus Anointing will also be charged with the rebuilding of Jerusalem. In this context, Jerusalem serves as a symbol representing the global Church of Jesus Christ. The Body of Christ is currently divided and fractured. That makes the Church very weak and ineffective in the earth.

We are unable to represent our Lord Jesus Christ as effective as we need to do. We are unable to be the salt of the earth and the light of the world in the true sense of the word. Because of this state of being divided and fractured, the Church is vulnerable to insidious practices and strange fire.

The Cyrus Anointing will rebuild the Church by fostering a culture of equipping the saints for the work of ministry for the edifying of the Body of Christ. The Cyrus Anointing will also build bridges between local churches as well as between denominations. The biggest part of this will be the massive financial commitment, to the rebuilding of the Church, made by those walking in the Cyrus Anointing.

Rebuilding the Temple

> *"That saith of Cyrus, He is my shepherd, and shall perform all my pleasure: even saying to Jerusalem, Thou shalt be built; and to the temple, Thy foundation shall be laid"* **(Isaiah 44:28).**

The fifth pillar or aspect of *The Mission of Cyrus* is the rebuilding of the Temple of God. In fact, this was the first thing that the Israelites that were freed by King Cyrus did when they arrived in Jerusalem. The most prominent person in the rebuilding of the Temple of God was Zerubbabel. Zerubbabel was not alone. He was with Jeshua. They continued the work under the prophetic ministry and encouragement of Haggai and Zechariah.

King Cyrus rebuilt the temple of God by issuing an irreversible decree, for the rebuilding of the temple of God, in accordance to the law of the Medes and Persians. He did not just end there but King Cyrus also gave the financial resources required for the rebuilding of the temple of God. He went even further than that by providing the blueprint for the temple as recorded in Ezra 6:3-5.

Now, the Cyrus Anointing being released today also has the same charge, mandate and assignment to rebuild the temple of God. In this context, the temple is symbolic of and represents the individual born again believer. Remember the Bible teaches us that our bodies are the temple of the Holy Spirit. It is for this reason that the Cyrus Anointing will not only focus on winning souls but will also be heavily financially committed in the holistic training and equipping of the believers.

This holistic training and equipping of believers will be characterised by regular and on-going workshops, seminars and conferences. It will even go further than just events into the establishment of cutting edge institutions and schools that equip believers holistically. The primary equipping will obviously be the spiritual equipping of the believers and that will be followed by the training and equipping of believers with skills that will help advance the specific believers in their specific callings.

Chapter Two

Cyrus – The Shepherd of the LORD

"That saith of Cyrus, He is my shepherd, and shall perform all my pleasure: even saying to Jerusalem, Thou shalt be built; and to the temple, Thy foundation shall be laid." **(Isaiah 44:28)**

In the above scripture quotation, God, through the mouth Isaiah the prophet refers to King Cyrus as "my shepherd". It is very interesting that God Almighty does not simply refer to King Cyrus as "a shepherd" but God takes full ownership of King Cyrus and calls him "my shepherd". This clearly distinguishes and sets King Cyrus apart from those shepherds that are self or man- made and establish him as a Shepherd assigned by God.

King Cyrus was a shepherd for whom God Almighty took full ownership. In other words, God Almighty Himself has birthed, called and commissioned King Cyrus' shepherding role and responsibility. It is God Himself that equipped King Cyrus for the role of being a shepherd.

In the Bible, the role of a shepherd mostly refers to leadership in its broad and various aspects and applications. There are shepherds that are in; government, judiciary, business, academia, family, church or religion, and many other spheres of life. The common thread that cuts throughout the different spheres and applications of shepherding is that all shepherds (leaders) are entrusted with the duty and responsibility of oversight over and ensuring the well-being of others.

There are two types of shepherds or leaders that I want to focus on. The true shepherds and the false shepherds. The true shepherds are those who are called, anointed and destined for it and the false shepherds are those who are motivated purely by self- interest and self-enrichment at the expense of those with whose well-being they are entrusted. Our Lord and Saviour, Jesus Christ of Nazareth gives us a lesson about these two types of leaders. In the gospel of John chapter 10, He says;

> *"Verily, verily, I say unto you, He that entereth not by the door into the sheepfold, but climbeth up some other way, the same is a thief and a robber. But he that entereth in by the door is the shepherd of the sheep. To him the porter openeth; and the sheep hear his voice: and he calleth his own sheep by name, and leadeth them out. And when he putteth forth his own sheep, he goeth before them, and the sheep follow him: for they know his voice. **(John 10v1-4)***

The self-serving shepherds access leadership roles and positions by pulling the proverbial strings, manipulation and manoeuvring themselves into such leadership positions. It is just like Jesus Christ teaches us, they do not enter by the door but they climb up some other way. They do this simply because they are driven by their greed, selfish ambition and love of honour that come from mere man.

As a result of these self-serving, self-appointed shepherds who "do not enter by the door", their incompetence and their lack of genuine concern and care for the well-being of those they shepherd surfaces. They are motivated by positions more than caring for the sheep.

The unfortunate thing is that most leadership roles come with access to certain opportunities and resources. Because of that access to such opportunities and resources, this breed of leaders begins to start serving their own interests at the expense of the "sheep". This is when they start thieving and robbing because deep down in their hearts, that is what they are. They are thieves and robbers.

Jesus Christ also teaches us that the one that enters by the door is the shepherd of the sheep. This is the authentic type of shepherds and leaders. The true shepherds or leaders, unlike the one discussed above, are not driven by self-interest, selfish ambition and greed. They are motivated by purpose, calling and their genuine love for the sheep. About true shepherds, the Bible says;

> *"And no man taketh this honour unto himself, but he that is called of God, as was Aaron. So also Christ glorified not himself to be made an high priest;..."* ***(Heb 5:4-6)***

This breed of shepherds or leaders does not take the honour unto themselves. They do not need to do any self-promotion none whatsoever. They wait on the LORD God Almighty to call them and bestow the honour on them. Unlike, the above leaders or shepherds, they do not have to scheme, manipulate and manoeuvre their way into leadership. They are disciples of Jesus Christ and because of that, they take their cue from Jesus Christ and emulate Him.

Because of this type of attitude and approach to leadership, the porter opens the gate to them. The porter in John 10v3 typifies the Holy Spirit. The Holy Spirit opens the gate to this breed of shepherd. The opening of the gates or doors denotes the favour of God that this breed of leaders will begin to experience in executing their shepherding responsibilities.

They do not have to toil or manipulate the "sheep". They also do not need to feel threatened by those they are leading or even feel insecure. Because they entered in by the door, they do not even have to convince, compel or manipulate the "sheep" into following them. This is because the "sheep" know and trust their voice because *"out of the abundance of the heart, the mouth speaks"*. The "sheep" trust their voice because they know the heart of this breed of shepherd. The sheep know that the shepherd has their best interest at heart.

King Cyrus, did not climb up some other way into the role of a shepherd. It is God Almighty Himself that birthed, called and commissioned King Cyrus to be a shepherd. There is no better entrance into leadership than being birthed, called and commissioned by God Himself into a leadership role. King Cyrus is this type or breed of shepherd that did not hijack the honour of God. The honour of God was bestowed upon King Cyrus by God Himself. The Bible attests to that and says;

> *"For the sake of Jacob my servant, of Israel my chosen, I summon you by name and **bestow on you a title of honor,......"** (Isaiah 45:v4 NIV).*

Because the entrance of King Cyrus into leadership is birthed, called and commissioned by God, he experienced the favour of God in executing his shepherding responsibilities. He did not need to convince, compel or manipulate the people he was assigned to lead into following him.

Taken literally, the role and responsibility of the shepherd is threefold. It is to lead, protect, and feed the sheep. In Psalm 23, King David gives us a very conspicuous and comprehensive picture of the role of the shepherd. He does this by referencing Thee Shepherd, the Chief Shepherd the LORD God Almighty as Shepherd.

The shepherd has the responsibility to lead and guide their sheep into a path that will result in the prosperity and wellness of the sheep. King David states of the LORD that; *"....he leadeth me beside the still waters. ....:he leadeth me in the paths of righteousness for his name's sake."* It is the duty of the shepherd to ensure that the flock entrusted to their care is led into a place of peace and doing that which is right all the time.

In executing their protective duty over the sheep, the shepherd is expected to put their own life on harm's way. We have seen this in the life of King David whilst he was a shepherd. A lion and a bear attacked his flock and David fought with and defeated both the lion and the bear only to save the one sheep that was captured by the lion and the one captured by the bear. Jesus Christ also teaches us this when He says; *"I am the good shepherd: the good shepherd giveth his life for the sheep" (John 10:11)*.

The other duty and responsibility of the shepherd is to feed the flock. David, also gives us a glimpse into this in Psalm 23. He says; *"The LORD is my shepherd; **I shall not want.......Thou preparest a table before me in the presence of mine enemies:...**"*. This is indeed the role of any true shepherd. After his resurrection, three times, Jesus Christ, told Peter; *"....,Feed my lambs........, Feed my sheep......, Feed my sheep" (John 21:17)*.

King Cyrus is this type of shepherd or leader. He is a shepherd and leader whom God charged with protecting His people, leading them out of Babylon back into their land and giving them provisions for the rebuilding of Jerusalem and the temple of the LORD. (2 Chronicles 36:22-23 and Ezra 1).

King Cyrus executed his shepherding or leadership responsibility faithfully. He *"performed all my pleasure"* when he conquered and spoiled Babylon and released an irreversible decree to rebuild the temple of God. The Bible tells us that;

> *"Now in the first year of Cyrus king of Persia, that the word of the LORD by the mouth of Jeremiah might be fulfilled, the LORD stirred up the spirit of*

36

*Cyrus king of Persia, that he made a proclamation throughout all his kingdom, and put it also in writing, saying, Thus saith Cyrus king of Persia, The LORD God of heaven hath given me all the kingdoms of the earth; and he hath charged me to build him an house at Jerusalem, which is in Judah. Who is there among you of all his people? His God be with him, and let him go up to Jerusalem, which is in Judah, and build the house of the LORD God of Israel, (he is the God,) which is in Jerusalem. And whosoever remaineth in any place where he sojourneth, let the men of his place help him with silver, and with gold, and with goods, and with beasts, beside the freewill offering for the house of God that is in Jerusalem." **(Ezra 1:1-4)***

King Cyrus performed the pleasure of God by going into war against Babylon, conquering it and freeing the Israelites from captivity and also issuing the irreversible decree to rebuild the temple of God. This engagement in war presented an obvious danger.

As a true shepherd, King Cyrus also led the children of Israel out of captivity back to their own land. He also led them back to reviving their covenant with God, resulting in the restoration of their relationship with God. This he did by issuing a decree that they should go back and rebuild the Temple of God and the city of God, Jerusalem. By doing this, King Cyrus led the Israelites in the paths of righteousness.

Lastly, King Cyrus executed his responsibility to feed the Israelites when he, not only restored to them the vessels and treasures that king Nebuchadnezzar had taken from the

Temple of God in Jerusalem, but he also decreed that vessels of silver, gold, goods, beasts and a free will offering be given to those that were returning to Jerusalem to rebuild the Temple of God.

In closing, this means that those who are called and anointed with the same grace and anointing that was on King Cyrus, the Cyrus Anointing, need to understand and embrace that they are called to leadership responsibility and not leadership position. The position is by default but the important thing is to understand, embrace and be faithful to the assignment and responsibility.

Being a shepherd requires lowliness of heart as it is not a glamorous job. It requires that a leader should be accessible and be willing to go to the lowliest of places and deal with the "lowliest" of people. This is made possible by a heart and mind that not only understands but also embraces the responsibility not just the position. It is those that understand that they are called to; lead, protect and feed the flock of God. These are the ones that will exhibit the shepherd's model of leadership expressed in the Cyrus Anointing.

It will also be very critical for the reader to seek the face of God so that He, by the Holy Spirit can reveal to them, the dominant sphere to which they are called to lead and shepherd the people of God. Remember, there are different spheres of leadership and shepherding such as government, business, academia, politics and others. That is why it becomes very fundamental that the reader knows the dominant one allocated to them by God Almighty.

King Cyrus was allocated not only the Medo-Persian geographic sphere to govern as their king but he also conquered and ruled over many more nations including Babylon. He was called into the government sphere. In today's release of the Cyrus Anointing, others will be called into government, entertainment, economics, academics, and many other spheres of leadership and influence.

Many presidents of nations will called and anointed with the Cyrus Anointing. We will not only see presidents but prime ministers, ministers, premiers, governors and mayors raised in the Cyrus Anointing. This will also be accompanied by presidents and chief executives of multi-national and listed blue chip companies being raised in the Cyrus Anointing. Not only that, we will see leaders in Education, Church, Entertainment and all other spheres raised in the Cyrus Anointing.

One of the key attributes of the Cyrus Anointing is noticeability and greatness. That is why those who are called with the Cyrus Anointing will be noticeable and established in greatness and dominance in their line of calling and assignment. Our calling into these spheres is to advance the Kingdom of God and have our Lord and Saviour, the King of kings, Jesus Christ of Nazareth worshipped.

As those called and anointed with the Cyrus Anointing, we have the responsibility to announce to Jerusalem (the Church of Jesus Christ) that: *"Thou shalt be built; and to the temple, Thy foundation shall be laid."* We have this awesome responsibility and duty to prophesy the above so that the Church is edified, exhorted and comforted.

It is also very critical that we remember that the New Testament temple is each and every believer that has received Jesus Christ and Jerusalem is the global Church of Jesus Christ.

Chapter Three

Cyrus – The Man of Righteousness

> *"Who raised up the righteous man from the east, called him to his foot, gave the nations before him, and made him rule over kings? He gave them as dust to his sword, and as driven stubble to his bow." (Isaiah 41:2)*

Again, God through the mouth of Isaiah, this time pronounces and calls King Cyrus, "the righteous man". It is a well-established fact that King Cyrus was a gentile and not one of the Israelites, yet God calls him "the righteous man".

Because of this reference to King Cyrus, one could easily think that this scripture ascribes righteousness to King Cyrus. One may even think that the scripture implies that King Cyrus was a believer in the God of Israel. On closer examination of the scriptures though, it becomes evident that King Cyrus did not have a relationship with Almighty God.

The Biblical evidence to this regard is found in Isaiah 45 and verse 5. The Bible tells us that;

> *"I am the LORD, and there is none else, there is no God beside me: I girded thee, <u>though hast not known me</u>:" (Isaiah 45:5)*

It is very evident in the above scripture that King Cyrus had no personal relationship with Jehovah God and therefore not a righteous person according to Biblical standards.

In relation to our opening scriptural passage the Benson Commentary of the Bible states the following;

"Cyrus might be called **a righteous man,** or, **a man of righteousness,** as the Hebrew rather means, because he was raised up **in righteousness,** as is said of him, and was God's great instrument, to manifest his **faithfulness** in fulfilling his promise of delivering his people out of Babylon, and his **justice** in punishing the enemies and oppressors of his people, the Babylonians;"

The Jamieson-Fausset-Brown Bible Commentary on the other hand states the following;

"the righteous man—Cyrus; as Isa 44:28; 45:1-4, 13; 46:11, "from the East," prove. Called "righteous," not so much on account of his own equity [Herodotus, 3.89], as because he fulfilled God's righteous will in restoring the Jews from their unjust captivity. Raised him up in righteousness. The Septuagint takes the Hebrew as a noun "righteousness." Maurer translates, "Who raised up him whom salvation (national and temporal, the gift of God's 'righteousness' to the good, Isa 32:17; compare Isa 45:8; 51:5) meets at his foot" (that is, wherever he goes)".

It is clear from both the Benson Commentary of the Bible and the Jamieson_Fausset_Brown Bible Commentary that King Cyrus was not necessarily a righteous man but he was raised up in righteousness by Almighty God. The New Living Translation of the Bible makes this clearer as it reads as follows;

> *"I will raise up Cyrus to fulfil my righteous purpose, and I will guide his actions. He will restore my city and free my captive people-without seeking a reward! I, the LORD of Heaven's Armies have spoken!"* ***(Isaiah 45:13).***

It is therefore evident that though King Cyrus himself was not righteous, he was raised and inspired by God to fulfil God's righteous purpose. That righteous purpose is that of restoring the city of God and freeing God's captive people.

One of the interesting things that we learn about King Cyrus is that he was aware that he was chosen and anointed by God. This awareness of being chosen and anointed by Almighty God is recorded in both 2 Chronicles 36 and Ezra 1. Both scriptures read as follows;

> *"Now in the first year of Cyrus king of Persia, that the word of the LORD spoken by the mouth of Jeremiah might be accomplished, the LORD stirred up the spirit of Cyrus king of Persia, that he made a proclamation throughout all his kingdom, and put it also in writing, saying, Thus saith Cyrus king of Persia, All the kingdoms of the earth hath the LORD God of heaven given me; and he hath charged me to build him an house in Jerusalem, which is in Judah. Who is there among you of all his people? The LORD*

his God be with him, and let him go up." *(2 Chronicles 36:22-23).*

*"Now in the first year of Cyrus king of Persia, that the word of the LORD spoken by the mouth of Jeremiah might be accomplished, the LORD stirred up the spirit of Cyrus king of Persia, that he made a proclamation throughout all his kingdom, and put it also in writing, saying, Thus saith Cyrus king of Persia, All the kingdoms of the earth hath the LORD God of heaven given me; and he hath charged me to build him an house in Jerusalem, which is in Judah. Who is there among you of all his people? The LORD his God be with him, and let him go up to Jerusalem, which is in Judah, and build the house of the LORD God of Israel, (he is the God,) which is in Jerusalem. And whosoever remaineth in any place where he sojourneth, let the men of his place help him with silver, and with gold, and with goods, and with beasts, beside the freewill offering for the house of God that is in Jerusalem." **(Ezra 1:1-4).***

This amazing level of awareness that King Cyrus had about his being chosen and anointed by God is testimony to yet another prophetic word that God spoke through Isaiah the prophet. That prophetic word reads as follows;

"I have raised up one from the north, and he shall come: ***from the rising of the sun shall he call upon my name:*** *and he shall come upon princes as upon morter, and as the porter treadeth clay."* ***(Isaiah 41:25)***

According to the above scripture quotation, King Cyrus called on the name of the LORD from the rising of the sun. In other words, King Cyrus attributed his victories and conquest to Jehovah God from the rising of the sun. He proclaimed the name of the God of Israel so much that he put the proclamation or decree in writing.

Now that we have Biblically established that King Cyrus was a man of righteous, I want to take some time and look at the righteous man aspect of the assignment of King Cyrus. Our introductory scripture text says; *"Who raised up the righteous man from the east, called him to his foot, gave the nations before him, and made him rule over kings? He gave them as dust to his sword, and as driven stubble to his bow."* **(Isaiah 41:2)**

Righteousness, service to God, victory over many nations and rulership over kings are four aspects of the assignment of Cyrus-The Man of Righteous that are worth noting. Now, let us look at these aspects in a more detailed manner;

Righteousness

Those who are called to walk in and manifest the Cyrus Anointing today also need to be righteous people. It means that they need to first and foremost be a people that believe in God (as per Romans 10:10) and are forever seeking to do that which is right and pleasing to Almighty God.

This is done by being reconciled to God by the blood of Jesus Christ. It is done by embracing and walking in their new identity in Jesus Christ. Unlike King Cyrus who did not know

Almighty God in a personal way, those called and anointed with the Cyrus Anointing will be born again by the Spirit of God. This breed of believers will be fuelled by having embraced that; *"For we are his workmanship, created in Christ Jesus unto good works, which God hath before ordained that we should walk in them." **(Ephesians 2:10)**.*

It is that faith in God that will enable believers to keep coming to Him and calling on Him from the rising of the sun. The importance of this cannot be overstated as continuously and faithfully calling on Him demonstrates their absolute dependence on Him.

Because of this approach and attitude of the heart, the LORD will lead them in the paths that they should walk in. He will lead them in the paths of righteousness. He will give them heavenly assignments to carry out in the earth and bring glory to His name. In reality, this is what will cause God to go before them and make the crooked places straight, break in pieces the gates of brass and cut in sunder the bars of iron and give unto them the treasures of darkness and the hidden riches of secret places.

Service to God

One of the key things made very clear in our scripture text is that King Cyrus was called to serve God. He was not called for the lime light and fame. This means that everything about his life, all his conquests, victories and successes were in service to Almighty God. None of it was about him gaining wealth, fame, dominance and popularity. It was about him performing the pleasure of Almighty God.

It is no different today for those called and anointed with the Cyrus Anointing. This breed of believers needs to die to self and be willing to serve God Almighty. This is going to take a great deal of sacrifice as they will be contending with the urgent necessities of life that will be screaming for their attention. All those called to walk in the Cyrus Anointing will be faced with difficult choices to make.

The choices will be between obeying God by doing His will and the demands of their everyday life. This is where they will have to choose between that which is expedient and that which has long lasting, multi-generational and eternal impact. That is why those called and anointed with the Cyrus Anointing need to be able to *"count the cost"* and be willing to lay down their lives to serve the will, counsel and purpose of God. They are to be men and women under God's authority.

In other words, they are to be a Matthew 6:33 people. They are to be a people that seek first the kingdom of God and His righteousness. There is no other way around this except whole-hearted surrender and reckless abandonment to the will and counsel of God. It is reaching the place that apostle Paul speaks about when he says; *"But we had the sentence of death in ourselves, that we should not trust in ourselves, but in God which raiseth the dead"* ***(2 Corinthians 1:9).***

Victory over many nations

According to our scripture text, God gave the nations to King Cyrus. This means that King Cyrus was given victory by Almighty God over many nations. It is Almighty God that determined the outcome of every battle and war that King Cyrus engaged in with the rest of the nations that he defeated. Remember the Bible says; *"not by might, nor by power b ut by My Spirit says the LORD of hosts."* ***(Zechariah 4:6)***

The New Testament believers that are called and anointed with the Cyrus Anointing will also experience victory over many nations. It is critical to remember 1 Peter 2:9 that says; *"But ye are a chosen generation, a royal priesthood,* ***an holy nation****, a peculiar people; that ye should show forth the praises of him who hath called you out of darkness into his marvellous light:.."*

According to the Bible, though this scripture primarily refers to the nation of Israel. New Testament believers are "an holy nation" by adoption through the Blood of Jesus Christ. They are a nation of those who are called out of darkness into the marvellous light of God. As the holy nation anointed with the Cyrus Anointing, they will also experience victory over many nations, those who are still in darkness and do not know Jesus Christ of Nazareth as their LORD and Saviour. There is a double-edged meaning of "victory over many nations". The one edge is spiritual whilst the other edge is physical.

The physical edge of the meaning translates to those called and anointed with the Cyrus Anointing displaying never seen before levels of competence, excellence and integrity and also walking in divine favour. It speaks of the manifest glory of God that is on the inside of them being fully displayed to an extent that, without trying to, they will outshine all the other "nations". This manifestation will far exceed Daniel, Hananiah, Mishael and Azariah being found to be ten times better than all the magicians and astrologers of Babylon (Daniel 1:20).

The spiritual edge translates to defeating these nations by winning them over to God's kingdom and bringing them under the authority of the LORD Jesus Christ of Nazareth. As a result of coming into an encounter with the above mentioned physical edge of victory over many nations, these "nations" will be drawn to the Light and inquire about how this breed of believers is able to walk in such excellence, favour, integrity, wisdom, wealth and competence. This will provide a door and an opportunity for them to testify about Jesus Christ. In this way, these "nations" will be reconciled to God.

Rulership over kings

It is a matter of both biblical and historical record that King Cyrus defeated and ruled over many kings including the king of Babylon. According to history, once he defeated a nation and their king, King Cyrus the Great, would let them retain their government on condition that they swore allegiance to him and also paid tribute money or colonial tax to him. This made him a ruler over an empire. Those he fought against didn't fight so desperately because they knew him to be a gracious victor.

The release of the Cyrus Anointing today will also see those endowed with the Cyrus Anointing ruling over kings. They will have rulership and dominion over the spiritual territorial demonic entities that have set and entrenched themselves as kings over the different geographical spheres as well as the different socio-economic and political spheres of life. They will be able to exercise authority and dominance over all hateful, ungodly and demonic entities. This will be a fulfilment of a physical and spiritual manifestation of Luke 10:19.

This rulership over kings will result in the freeing of nations, regions and continents from satanic manipulation, control and dominance. It will result in the reclaiming of all spheres of life including politics, economies, families, academics, entertainment and other spheres. These spheres will be realigned and brought under the Lordship of Jesus Christ of Nazareth.

Because of this, the vicious grip of the enemy over the nations and peoples of the earth will be severely broken and completely weakened. The natural outcome of this is that, the devil will no longer be able to deceive the nations and blind their eyes. It will be a season and a time of open eyes and ears that will result in the peoples of the earth seeing the goodness of God and hearing His Word. The peoples of the earth will be receptive to the Word of God. An unparalleled harvest of souls into the kingdom of God will be seen.

Lastly, as a righteous man, King Cyrus is a man that calls on the name of the LORD from the rising of the sun. He was a man that proclaimed the Name of God and attributed all his conquests and victories to Him. This posture of magnifying God and giving glory to Him earned him unparalleled favour with God. It is this posture that saw him given victory over many nations as well as dominion over many kings. This is the portion of those called and anointed with the same grace and anointing as the one that was on King Cyrus.

Chapter Four

Cyrus – the Ravenous Bird

"Calling a ravenous bird from the east, the man that executeth my counsel from a far country: yea, I have spoken it, I will also bring it to pass; I have purposed it, I will also do it" **(Isaiah 46v11)**

"From the east I summon a bird of prey; from a far off land, a man to fulfil my purpose. What I have said, that will I bring about; what I have planned, that will I do." **(Isaiah 46v11 NIV)**

God refers to King Cyrus as the ravenous bird. The New International Version of the Bible refers to King Cyrus as the bird of prey. Now, a bird of prey is a hunting bird. It feeds on other animals. It is a carnivorous bird. Granted, there are different types of birds of prey. The Message translation of the Bible reads as follows; *"Calling that eagle, Cyrus out of the east, from a far country the man I chose to help me. I've said it, and I'll most certainly do it. I've planned it, so it's as good as done.*

Birds of prey share most of their characteristics and attributes. I think, it is safe to adopt the eagle as the subject bird of prey as we decode Cyrus the Ravenous Bird. Having said that, I want us to take a look at some of the characteristics and attributes of the Ravenous Bird.

The characteristics and traits of ravenous birds include the following; keen vision, hunger for gratification, ferocious, exceptional flight abilities, strong feet for holding prey, strong talons for catching and killing the prey, eats vertebrates and a strong beak for tearing the flesh of their prey. Now, let us look at what these mean for the Cyrus Anointing.

Keen Vision

Birds of prey possess a very keen vision. This keen vision of theirs enables them to detect their prey during flight. You must remember that birds of prey fly at very high altitudes even though they mostly feed on the ground. Whilst they are on the ground, it is difficult for them to be able to see their prey. So, the higher they fly the easier it becomes for them to spot their prey.

Eagles are able to spot a moving prey on the ground during flight. Once, they spot the moving prey on the ground, they are able to calculate their speed and angle of descent so as to catch the prey at a different spot than when the eagle spotted the prey during flight.

This is a defining attribute and trait for those called and anointed with the Cyrus Anointing. Those called and anointed with the Cyrus Anointing are visionary leaders. They are never ever content with the status quo. They are not necessarily ambitious more than they are visionaries. Their vision is refined, perfected and clarified in prayer. The more they pray, the clearer their vision becomes. This is because the source of their vision is God Almighty Himself. They don't just have ambitious and carnal ideas. They download the counsel of God from their time of intimacy and fellowship with God.

Just like an eagle is able to calculate its speed and angle of descent when its approaching a moving prey so will those anointed with the Cyrus Anointing be strategic in the implementation of their God given visions. The Cyrus Anointing is a very strategic and calculative anointing.

Other business men and women called and anointed with the Cyrus Anointing will receive visions from God to take over going concerns. Such going concerns could be companies listed on the securities exchanges. They will be given grace and ability to take over entire listed companies. They will know exactly how to approach the takeover of such corporations.

For those desiring to walk in the Cyrus Anointing, I want to advise them that prayer and fasting should become a part of your life. Obviously, the continual searching of the Scriptures forms a fundamental part of their prayer and fasting. If they are not prepared to put in the time through Word study, prayer and fasting; then they might as well forget now about experiencing the fullness of the Cyrus Anointing in their life.

It is my advice to them, that they get themselves books and tapes on prayer and fasting. Read these books and listen to the teaching tapes. Don't get me wrong, by spending time in prayer and fasting, they are not going to move the hand of

God but they are merely equipping themselves for the battle ahead.

Remember that the devil has entrenched himself in the marketplace by bringing seven other devils more wicked than himself. This took place when some well-meaning but ignorant former generations of Church leadership preached against the marketplace. They taught and preached that it was evil for believers to get involved in politics, business, academics and all other spheres of life.

As a result of their teaching and preaching most saints forsook the marketplace and that created a vacuum for the devil to occupy. This is the kind that Jesus Christ says; it will not go out except by prayer and fasting. If those called and anointed with the Cyrus Anointing are going to remove and unseat ancient principalities, they will need to be spiritually and mentally fit for the battle. It is for this that prayer and fasting are fundamental as the devil is not going to simply relinquish the marketplace but will put up a fight.

Hunger for Gratification

A Ravenous Bird is a bird that is greedy and hungry for gratification. It goes after its prey with all its strength and might. It is committed to catching the prey at whatever the cost. There is no fear or doubt in the mind of a ravenous bird as it approaches its prey. The only objective that occupies the mind of a ravenous bird is that it is hungry and that it is going to eat and be filled after it has caught its prey.

This is the same attitude and mind-set that was in King Cyrus as he attacked, captured and destroyed Babylon. The only thing that was on his mind was the end of it all. His mind was on accomplishing the counsel of Almighty God concerning the nation of Babylon. King Cyrus was hasty in dealing with the Babylonians.

That is why the Cyrus Anointing today is an anointing that is results driven. Those anointed with the Cyrus Anointing are hungry to see results. All what they want to see is the rule of Almighty God established in every single domain in the face of the earth. They will not rest until the rule of God is established in all the institutions of the earth and in all the sectors of the economy and the society. They are greedy for the establishment of the Kingdom of Heaven in the earth and the reign of Jesus Christ.

Birds of Prey Are Ferocious

Birds of prey are ferocious. They are combative birds. They are not afraid of engaging in a fight. They are fierce and equipped for a fight. Birds of prey do not back down from a fight. They are vicious and do not relent. They fight hard for the prey, their meal.

Birds of prey are violent in their nature. This attribute is the same with those called and anointed with the Cyrus Anointing. They exhibit extreme levels of spiritual violence and intolerance against the devil. They attack the devil in whatever form he may manifest himself. The Cyrus Anointing is a proponent for justice, fairness and equality. It gets stirred up very quickly when such elements of injustice, inequality, unfairness and oppression are manifested.

This is the breed that lays hold of the Kingdom of heaven. It is the breed that is described by Jesus Christ when he says; *"And from the days of John the Baptist until now the kingdom of heaven suffereth violence, and the violent take it by force." (Matthew 11v12).* This breed of believers doesn't take any chances. They know that the devil is the enemy of their souls. They have internalized John 10v10.

Because of this, they do not play games. They terminate the devil's schemes, with extreme prejudice and with the contempt he deserves, wherever he manifest himself. They are vigilant in their conduct just like an eagle that attacks a prey that is much larger than itself in size. The eagle understands that there is no room for error or being nice to its prey. It knows that one mistake from itself; it could end up a prey itself. That is why the Cyrus Anointing submits itself to God. In that way, it is able to resist the devil.

Exceptional Flight Abilities

An eagle possesses exceptional flight abilities. It is able to perform amazing acrobatic manoeuvres whilst it is in flight. Its navigational abilities are also very exceptional. Eagles also fly at the highest altitudes. They even make their nests in very high and not so easily accessible places. Eagles make their nests in the mountains and on the cliffs.

This is one of the key attributes of the Cyrus Anointing today. Those anointed with the Cyrus Anointing will be able to engage in prayer. As a result of that, they will reach different dimensions of prayer and pray all kinds of prayers. This is because they are so yielded to the Holy Spirit and the Holy Spirit carries them just like an eagle gets carried by the wind.

Being yielded to the Holy Spirit will enable those called and anointed with the Cyrus Anointing to navigate the realms of the spirit. As they do that, they will receive their instructions and mandate from the presence of God Almighty.

Strong Feet for Holding Prey

Eagles have very strong feet. Their feet are utilised for holding their prey. An eagle pounces on its prey and uses its feet to hold down the prey. Once the feet of the eagle get hold of the prey, there is no getting out of that grip for the prey. The grip is so strong and the feet of the eagle are used to pin the prey to the ground and to stomp on it until it dies.

Walking in the authority of Luke 10:19 will be a reality for those anointed with the Cyrus Anointing. They will trample on serpents and scorpions and over all the power of satan and nothing shall by any means be able to hurt them.

As a result of walking in the full manifestation of Luke 10:19; they will also hold fast to the territories that they have taken over. They will firmly entrench themselves in every single domain that God Almighty entrusts them with. The Cyrus Anointing will establish a system of governance and administration that is water tight. This will ensure that the will of God concerning that particular domain never gets diluted or compromised.

Strong Talons for Catching and Killing the Prey

Once an eagle has its talons on its prey, it doesn't let go of that prey. The grip of those talons is so tight. The talons draw blood from the prey of the eagle. It is also these very talons that the eagle uses to kill its prey.

The Cyrus Anointing is equipped with the same abilities that enable it to "sink its claws" on its target. It is very violent in dealing with its target. Of course this violence is a spiritual violence when engaging in spiritual warfare.

Eats Vertebrates

An eagle hunts and eats vertebrates. These are animals that are much larger in size than the eagle itself. It is also for that reason that an eagle has very strong legs, very strong talons and a very strong beak. It is because; the eagle hunts and eat prey that is much larger than itself.

The Cyrus Anointing revels in tackling situations that seem to be impossible. Where others see problems and challenges, the Cyrus Anointing sees an opportunity. Those called and anointed with the Cyrus Anointing have a problem of not knowing the phrase, 'start small'. This is because their wiring and design is for massive undertakings. The Cyrus Anointing loves to bring down Goliaths.

A Very Strong Beak

An eagle has a very strong beak. It uses its beak to tear apart the flesh of the prey when it is feeding.

The Cyrus Anointing is also very strong in issuing apostolic decrees and prophetic declarations. It is with these apostolic decrees and prophetic declarations that the Cyrus Anointing will tear apart the work of the devil. It is with these decrees and declarations that whole nations and cities will be delivered. The powers of darkness that control nations, regions, cities, industries and other domains will be torn down by the issuing of these decrees and declarations.

It is very important that the apostolic decrees and prophetic declarations issued proceed from the Word of God. Because of that, they are a sword of the Spirit that tears apart and dispel all darkness.

Executing the Counsel of God – Executive Authority

God calls king Cyrus *"...the man that executeth my counsel from a far country..."*. This means that King Cyrus had the honour of carrying out all that which was in the mind of God concerning Babylon and other nations that were given to him by God. King Cyrus was like an obedient soldier that receives its orders and carries them out. The beautiful thing about King Cyrus is that he received his orders directly from God Almighty.

This is the privilege and honour that is afforded to the Cyrus Anointing today. It is the honour of receiving its instructions and orders directly from God Almighty. It is the privilege and honour of being privy to the thoughts of God Almighty. This is not just knowing the thoughts of God but also playing an active role in the fulfilment of the plan and purpose of God in the earth today.

In closing, once again, I cannot emphasize enough that those desiring to walk in the Cyrus Anointing must develop an intimate relationship with God by means of prayer and the studying of the Word. There is no substitute for an intimate relationship with God. Failure to develop such a relationship means that you will not be able to hear the voice of God. If you cannot hear the voice of God how can you possibly know what is on His mind? If you do not know what the counsel of God is, how can you possibly execute it?

Developing this relationship is going to take some sacrifice on your part. There will be things and people that you must let go off in your life. Your priorities will change significantly. God requires that that which is important to us dies so that that which is important to Him can live. God requires that you sacrifice your Isaac. Sacrifice and let go of the thing that is closest to your heart.

Chapter Five

Cyrus - the Anointed One

Anointing

> *"Thus saith the LORD to his anointed, to Cyrus, whose right hand I have holden, to subdue nations before him; and I will loose the loins of kings, to open before him the two leaved gates; and the gates shall not be shut; I will go before thee, and make the crooked places straight: I will break in pieces the gates of brass, and cut in sunder the bars of iron: And I will give thee the treasures of darkness, and hidden riches of secret places, that thou mayest know that I, the LORD, which call thee by thy name, am the God of Israel. For Jacob my servant's sake, and Israel mine elect, I have even called thee by thy name: I have surnamed thee, though thou hast not known me. I am the LORD, and there is none else, there is no God beside me: I girded thee, though thou hast not known me: That they may know from the rising of the sun, and from the west, that there is none beside me. I am the LORD, and there is none else"* **(Isaiah 45v1-6)**.

In the above scripture quotation we learn that through Isaiah, God refers to King Cyrus as "his anointed". Now, I want us to take a bit of time and look at what it means to "anoint".

To anoint means "to smear upon or rub with oil". The physical smearing upon or rubbing with oil is an external acknowledgement of the fact that the one being anointed is commissioned by God. It is a symbolic representation that one is chosen by the LORD God Almighty for a specific divine assignment, task and mandate from God.

Like I said before, the act of physically smearing oil upon and anointing a person is an external acknowledgment of what God has already decided, done and established. It is meant to; publicly commission the person being anointed, equip and set them apart for the mandate that God Almighty has already given them. We see several examples of this in the bible such as when both Saul and David were anointed kings of Israel and Judah respectively. The Bible says;

> *"Then Samuel took a vial of oil, and poured it upon his head, and kissed him, and said, Is it not because the LORD hath anointed thee to be captain over his inheritance?"* **(1 Samuel 10v1)**

> *"Then Samuel took the horn of oil, and anointed him in the midst of his brethren: and the Spirit of the LORD came upon David from that day forward."* **(1 Samuel 16v13)**

The Purpose and Function of the Anointing

At this point, I want us to take a look at the general purpose and function of the anointing. Now, the purpose of the anointing is vast and limitless. For the purpose of our study, I will quote only two scriptures that give us a glimpse into the purpose and function of the anointing. After that, we will take some time and look at the specific function and purpose of the Cyrus Anointing.

The Anointing Removes Burdens and Destroys Yokes

The Bible says;

> *"And it shall come to pass in that day, that his burden shall be taken away from off thy shoulder, and his yoke from off thy neck, and the yoke shall be destroyed because of the anointing."* ***(Isaiah 10v27)***
>
> *"How God anointed Jesus of Nazareth with the Holy Ghost and with power: who went about doing good, and healing all that were oppressed of the devil; for God was with him."* ***(Acts 10v38)***

The anointing removes burdens. It also destroys yokes. Now burdens and yokes come in different shapes, sizes and manifestations. The very objective of burdens and yokes is to wear people down. They are tools that satan uses to subdue, dominate and oppress the people of God.

As we can see in Acts 10v38 quoted above, burdens and yokes manifested themselves through sicknesses, demon possession and many various other ills. Such various ills can be caused by spirits of; depression, suicide, suspicion, anger, paranoia, witchcraft and many others.

These burdens and yokes are brought about by the devil. Remember, Jesus Christ says, *"The thief cometh not but for to steal, and to kill, and to destroy:.." (John 10v10)*. That is why the Bible teaches that; *"....we wrestle not against flesh and blood but against principalities, against powers, against the rulers of the darkness of this world, against spiritual wickedness in high places." (Ephesians 6v12)*.

Though these burdens and yokes may appear to be physical, in reality they are not. They are more spiritual than physical. Actually, they are a physical manifestation of a spiritual state and condition. Hence it is the purpose and function of the anointing to remove these burdens and destroy these yokes. Remember, the anointing is not physical. It is the manifestation of the Holy Spirit.

Now, Jesus Christ says of Himself; *"I am come that they might have life, and that they might have it more abundantly." (John 10v10)*. The result of having burdens removed and yokes destroyed is life, abundant life. It is Jesus Christ that removes our burdens and destroys our yokes. The word "Christ" means "the anointed one and His anointing". That is why Jesus Christ says; *"Come unto me, all ye that labour and are heavy laden, and I will give you rest." (Matthew 11v28)*.

Freedom and liberty from burdens and yokes is the work of the anointing. Furthermore, it is impossible to access the anointing without Jesus Christ (Jesus - the Anointed One and His Anointing). We know this because John the Baptist testifies about Jesus Christ and says, *"...I saw the Spirit descending from heaven like a dove, and it abode upon him. And I knew him not: but he that sent me to baptize with water, the same said unto me, Upon whom thou shalt see the Spirit descending, and remaining on him, the same is he which baptizeth with the Holy Ghost." (John 1v32-33).*

When we have the anointing in our lives, then we have the power and ability to remove burdens and destroy yokes. After all, Jesus Christ says; *"But ye shall receive power, after that the Holy Ghost is come upon you:..." (Acts 1v8).* Now, this particular purpose and function of the anointing is demonstrated many times in the Bible but I want to relate one particular scripture text that depicts the removal of burdens and destroying of yokes.

Zechariah 1v18-21 says; *"Then lifted up I mine eyes, and saw, and behold four horns. And I said unto the angel that talked with me, What be these? And he answered me, These are the horns which scattered Judah, Israel and Jerusalem. And the LORD shewed me four carpenters. Then said I, What come these to do? And he spake, saying, These are the horns which have scattered Judah, so that no man did lift up his head: but these are come to fray them, to cast out the horns of the Gentiles, which lifted up their horn over the land of Judah to scatter it."*

Obviously the background of this scripture is about four other nations that had overpowered and subdued Judah, Israel and Jerusalem. What Zechariah sees is a vision of these four horns as well as four carpenters whom God would use to destroy these four horns that were subduing and oppressing Judah.

This is a perfect picture of how God prepared four anointed carpenters that would each confront, defeat and completely destroy one of the four horns. This gets me to conclude that different people are anointed for different and specific assignments (burdens and yokes). Otherwise God could have used one carpenter to confront, defeat and completely destroy all four horns.

The anointing removes burdens and destroys yokes. I hope and trust that the above captures and clarifies the purpose and function of the anointing, in as far as removing burdens and destroying yokes is concerned, not completely but sufficiently enough for you to understand this particular purpose and function of the anointing.

The Anointing Teaches Us

The Bible says;

> *"But the anointing which ye have received of him abideth in you, and ye need not that any man teach you: but as the same anointing teacheth you of all things, and is truth, and is no lie, and even as it hath taught you, ye shall abide in him."* **(1 John 2v27)**

The anointing teaches us. It is very important to remember that, without the Holy Spirit, there is no anointing. It is impossible to divorce the anointing from the Holy Spirit. As mentioned before, to anoint is to endow someone with supernatural ability. Obviously that anointing or supernatural ability comes from a particular source. In our case, the source is Jesus Christ of Nazareth the Son of the Most High God.

I believe that the anointing or supernatural ability comes from different sources because the Bible teaches us that; *"...God anointed Jesus of Nazareth with the Holy Ghost and with power:..." (Acts10v38)*. Jesus Christ was anointed specifically with the Holy Ghost and with power. It is also important that we remember the words of Jesus Christ to His disciples where he says; *"But you shall receive power after that the Holy Ghost is come upon you:..." (Acts 1v8)*.

One of the key things that Jesus Christ says about the Holy Spirit is; *"But the Comforter, which is the Holy Ghost, whom the Father will send in my name, he shall teach you all things, and bring all things to your remembrance, whatsoever I have said unto you." (John 14v26)*.

Now, the main issue that John is addressing in 1 John2 v 18-27 is how the anointing we have received from Jesus Christ enables us to discern between what is real and what is counterfeit. John is talking about how the anointing enables us to identify the antichrists. As stated in the Bible, the antichrist is anyone that denies that Jesus Christ was born by a virgin woman and lived among man as a child and grew up like any other human being.

It is the anointing that enables us to discern the real from the counterfeit. The importance of this function and purpose of the anointing cannot be overstated or overemphasized in these days that we are living in. It is very difficult to ignore the surge in the number of counterfeit ministries in our days. This is exactly why it is ever increasingly critical to be vigilant and ensure that we allow the anointing of the Holy Ghost to teach us.

I think it is also very important that I make mention of the fact that there is no anointing without power. The anointing is normally demonstrated by supernatural ability. As mentioned earlier, to anoint means to endow or equip someone with supernatural ability. Even Jesus Christ told us about receiving power once we are anointed with the Holy Ghost (Acts 1v8).

The Cyrus Anointing

At this point, I want to take some time and look at how the above two functions or purposes of the anointing apply to the Cyrus Anointing.

The Cyrus Anointing Removes Burdens and Destroys Yokes

> *"I have raised him up in righteousness, and I will direct all his ways: he shall build my city, <u>and he shall let go my captives</u>, not for price nor reward, saith the LORD of hosts." (Isaiah 45v13)*

As mentioned before, one of the fundamental reasons for the release of an anointing is for the removal of burdens and the destruction of yokes. King Cyrus was anointed to remove the burden that the king of Babylon had placed on the Israelites. He was also anointed to destroy the yoke of the king of Babylon upon the people of God.

As mentioned in Isaiah 45v13, King Cyrus was anointed to *let go my captives.* He was called and anointed to free the captive Israelites from a Babylonian slavery, dominion and oppression. Remember, Israel was removed from their land and enslaved in Babylon. Cyrus was anointed and equipped by God to go into Babylon and capture Babylon in order to free Israel.

Ancient Babylon is a figure, symbol and prophetic shadow of today's world's system. It is a prophetic shadow of the kosmos. The world is a life and livelihood that is completely independent of God. It is actually a promotion of self-sufficiency and self-reliance while completely excluding God. It is a system of humanism that is anti-God.

The Cyrus Anointing Teaches Us

I think it is very important that we firstly establish that the proper and appropriate location of the Cyrus Anointing is under the Lordship of Jesus Christ of Nazareth. Remember, our fundamental scripture in as far as the anointing teaching us relates to discerning the anti-Christ.

Other people, out of fear or ignorance might want to argue that Cyrus was a gentile and therefore could not acknowledge Jesus Christ as LORD of Lords and KING of kings. Whilst it is okay to be cautious, it is more important to remember that greater is He that is in us than he that is in the world. With that said, I want to point out that, though he was a gentile, King Cyrus was raised and anointed by God. The Bible says;

> *"I have raised up one from the north, and he shall come: <u>from the rising of the sun shall he call upon my name</u>: and he shall come upon princes as upon*

> morter, and as the porter treadeth clay." (Isaiah 41v25)

It is very clear and evident from the above scripture quotation that King Cyrus attributed all his victories to Jehovah God as mentioned in 2 Chronicles 36 and Ezra 1. The Bible says he did this from the rising of the sun. In other words, King Cyrus announced from the east that all his conquest and victories were given to him by God and gave God the pre-eminence that He deserves. By continually doing this, King Cyrus placed himself at God's disposal and in a place where he would be entrusted with more victories and conquests by God.

Now, let us take a look at the Cyrus Anointing teaching us. The Bible says;

> "I have raised him up in righteousness, <u>and I will direct all his ways</u>: he shall build my city, and he shall let go my captives, not for price nor reward, saith the LORD of hosts." (Isaiah 45v13)

We have already established through Scripture that one of the key functions of the anointing is teaching. In the above quoted Scripture we can clearly see that God says He will direct all of Cyrus' ways. If we continually yield ourselves to the LORD, then the LORD will continue to unveil the depth, length, breadth and height of the Cyrus Anointing.

We will be taught how to walk in this anointing. We will be taught how to apply this anointing. The Cyrus Anointing will teach us about the specific industries, sectors and mountains of our Godly assignments. The Cyrus Anointing will teach us how to prosper and overcome in the sectors and industries of our assignment.

For an example, I once asked God; "LORD, exactly what do you mean when you say we are to make disciples of the nations? Is making disciples of the nations merely limited to preaching and getting people saved and filled with the Holy Ghost? Is that all there is to this Great Commission of making disciples of the nations?"

The LORD's response to me was both revelatory and astounding. His response was;

> "That is part of it but it is merely the beginning. Consider a man that I have called and placed in a parliamentary portfolio committee of foreign affairs for instance. This person will spend time in My Presence and seek My Face. Through this person's fellowship with Me, I will then download a draft foreign affairs policy to them.
>
> Once this person takes and presents this draft policy I have given to him/her, it will be widely accepted without any resistance because it will be so clear and address all concerns."

After this the LORD took me to the book of Isaiah where the Bible says;

> *"Who raised up the righteous man from the east, called him to his foot, and gave the nations before him, and made him rule over kings? He gave them as dust to his sword, and as driven stubble to his bow.*

> *He pursued them, and passed safely; even by the way that he had not gone with his feet." **(Isaiah 41v2-3)***

The LORD pointed out to me that when you take a sword and strike against dust, there is absolutely no resistance. There is absolutely no contest. That is why the draft foreign affairs policy is received without any resistance.

Those that are endued and anointed with the Cyrus Anointing will experience the same victories within their fields of divine assignments. Their fields of divine assignment will be diverse and include but not be limited to; church, the business world, engineering field, medical field, government, legal professions and all other spheres. The only requirement is that they remain faithful to God and not be lazy to spend time with God.

Before closing this chapter, I want to take some time and provide more detail about what the Cyrus Anointing is really about.

The Cyrus Anointing is Executive Authority

> *"Calling a ravenous bird from the east, the man that <u>executeth</u> my counsel from a far country:..." **(Isaiah 46:11)***

Those who are called and anointed with the Cyrus Anointing are graced and equipped with the ability to carry out the plans and purposes of God in the earth. Obviously, they will not carry out and execute all the plans and purposes of God but only those that are revealed and assigned to them to execute by God.

In the case of King Cyrus that plan and purpose was the destruction of ancient Babylon. He carried and executed that plan faithfully. Those whom God is raising to walk in the present-day Cyrus Anointing will need to discern the plans and purposes of God that are assigned to them.

Knowing and faithfully embracing the plans and purposes of God assigned to them is the only way that the executive authority will be released.

The Cyrus Anointing is the anointing of a "Sent One"

> *"Thus saith the LORD, your redeemer, the Holy One of Israel; For your sake I have sent to Babylon, and have brought down all their nobles, and the Chaldeans, whose cry is in the ships."* ***(Isaiah 43:14)***

The lives of those called, raised and anointed to walk in and manifest present-day Cyrus Anointing will characterised by a deep sense of a mission and assignment. They will be a people that did not just get up and go but they will be sent by God Almighty.

In other words, their assignment and calling will be apostolic in nature. To be apostolic means; "to be sent to a specific place with a specific assignment wherein the sent one assumes the authority of the One that sent them" ***(Paraphrase of Apostle John Eckhardt's definition of apostolic)***.

This means that, they will operate like ambassadors. Once an ambassador speaks, they articulate the position of their home country and their statements are regarded as the official position of their home country. Those called, raised and anointed with the Cyrus Anointing will articulate the position of heaven.

The Cyrus Anointing is a Building Anointing

> *"That saith of Cyrus, He is my shepherd, and shall perform all my pleasure: even saying to Jerusalem, Thou shalt be built; and to the temple, Thy foundation shall be laid."* **(Isaiah 44:28)**

Resident within the Cyrus Anointing is the grace to build. This is but one of the many different divine endowments that are resident within the Cyrus Anointing. This is the grace and ability to build accurately and to build according to blueprints.

The Cyrus Anointing does not build with the same bricks from the rubble of Babylon. Those that are called to walk in and manifest the Cyrus Anointing will not build with the principles and policies of Babylon. That is why the Bible says; *"And they shall not take of thee a stone for a corner, nor a stone for foundations; but thou shalt be desolate for ever, saith the LORD. "* **(Jeremiah 51:26)**.

Building with the Cyrus Anointing is to build as a wise master builder. This means that those who are called to walk in and manifest the Cyrus Anointing will not take things for granted and recycle the bricks of Babylon. They will patiently wait on the LORD so that He can reveal to them the stones that they are to use in building.

The Cyrus Anointing is a Strategic Anointing

> *"A drought is upon her waters; and they shall be dried up: for it is the land of graven images, and they are mad upon their idols." **(Jeremiah 50:38)***

King Cyrus was a formidable military strategist. That is why when he came against Babylon he redirected the water supply away from the city of Babylon.

This resulted in a famine gripping the city of Babylon. As a result of this famine, the Babylonians (King, princes, officers, army and civilians) grew weaker by the day.

It is because of the employment of this strategy by King Cyrus that enabled him to conquer Babylon very easily.

Those called to walk in and manifest the Cyrus Anointing need to understand that strategic thinking, strategic planning, strategic praying and strategic actions are a critical part of the Cyrus Anointing.

It is important to remember that the Bible says; "Counsel in the heart of man is like deep waters; but a man of understanding will draw it out." (Proverbs 20:5).

Through strategic thinking and strategic praying, they will be able to draw out the counsel of God from deep within them. The counsel of God will ensure that they have the perfect approach in taking over in the government, business, academia and all other spheres of the marketplace.

As seen in the capture of Babylon, that Babylon was captured and overthrown without a fight; so will employing God given strategies enable the Cyrus Anointing carriers of today to bring down enormous demonic entities very easily. (Daniel 5:30-31).

Unusual Wealth is a By Product and Confirmation of the Cyrus Anointing

> *"For Jacob my servant's sake, and Israel mine elect, I have even called thee by thy name: I have surnamed thee, though thou hast not known me."* ***(Isaiah 45:4)***
>
> *"Thus saith the LORD, your redeemer, the Holy One of Israel; For your sake I have sent to Babylon, and have brought down all their nobles, and the Chaldeans, whose cry is in the ships."* ***(Isaiah 43:14)***

Most people make the mistake of thinking that the Cyrus Anointing is about getting wealth. As a result of that their motivation and pursuit becomes defiled as they begin to focus on the material things and pursue financial gain. Many are driven by the love of money and the Mammon spirit.

Because God is not in what these people are pursuing, they find themselves toiling and struggling without any measure of success. If they exhibit success, then it is success that is achieved due to their humanistic efforts, schemes and hustling.

The aim of the Cyrus Anointing is to free the people of God that are held captive in Babylonian captivity. It is also to execute God's judgment over the ungodly and evil systems of the world just like King Cyrus completely destroyed historic Babylon.

The wealth and treasures are given by God to those that are actively engaging in the destruction of Babylon and the freeing of those who are trapped and enslaved in Babylon. The wealth and treasures are not something that those anointed with the Cyrus Anointing will chase after and pursue but something that is given to them by God as a confirmation of the call of God.

In conclusion, those who are called by God and endowed with the Cyrus Anointing have the same duty, mandate and assignment. They are tasked with the removal of the burdens that the devil places on the people of God. They are tasked to destroy the yoke of the devil that is not giving the people of God rest. They are called to deliver the people of God from the world's system that is anti-God. You may be asking, "How will the Cyrus Anointing accomplish this"? The Bible says;

> "....For your sake I have sent to Babylon, and have brought down all their nobles, and the Chaldeans, whose cry is in the ships." (Isaiah 43v14)

Isaiah 43v14 lets us know that God sent King Cyrus into Babylon to bring down all their nobles. The nobles were all their rulers. It is critical to remember that, *we wrestle not against flesh and blood, but against principalities, against powers, against the rulers of the darkness of this world, against spiritual wickedness in high places".*

The release of the Cyrus Anointing today will see all these; principalities, powers, rulers of the darkness of this world and spiritual wickedness in high places brought down. They will be stripped off of their control and power over and against the people of God. These are demonic entities that have set themselves over cities, regions and nations that will be subdued by the Cyrus Anointing to a place wherein they flee.

Once people are delivered and set free by the Cyrus Anointing, they will begin to pursue the will, counsel and purpose of God concerning their lives. We will see the people of God coming together and rebuilding the temple of God just like those whom King Cyrus delivered in the book of Ezra.

They will seek the face of God and join themselves to the LORD in a perpetual covenant.

Now, New Testament believers that are called to walk in and endowed with the Cyrus Anointing are also to be properly aligned and located under the Lordship of Jesus Christ of Nazareth. They are those that believe and agree that Jesus Christ was born of a virgin woman and grew up as man.

As New Testament believers, they do not need that oil should be smeared on them before they can walk in the Cyrus Anointing. This anointing is already within those whom God Almighty has chosen for them to walk in it. In other words, it is not a requirement to have oil physically smeared on them in order to walk in this anointing.

All that is required is for that same anointing to be activated by them sitting under and associating with ministries that teach, preach and demonstrate the Cyrus Anointing. This is one of the key manners in which any anointing, including the Cyrus Anointing, gets imparted. Remember the Bible says; *"Faith comes by hearing and hearing by the word of God". (Hebrew 6v6)*

Lastly, it is because of the Cyrus Anointing that God strengthens the right hand of those called and anointed with the Cyrus Anointing. Because of the Cyrus Anointing He will: subdue nation before those carrying this anointing; loose the loins of kings and cause them (kings) to be favourably disposed to those with the Cyrus Anointing; and open gates before the Cyrus Anointing giving them free reign and access; make the crooked places straight; break in pieces the gates of brass and cut in sunder bars of iron and usher the Cyrus Anointing into treasures of darkness and hidden riches of secret places.

These treasures of darkness and hidden riches of secret places are actual physical treasures such as gold, diamonds silver and other precious metals and stones. These are treasures that are hidden by the wealthiest people in the world because of tax evasion and also because some of them were acquired by extra legal means.

I know this because for starters, it was physical treasures and riches that king Nebuchardnezzar stole from Jerusalem and Judah and hid in dark secret places. I also know that because early this year (2018) the LORD showed me a dream wherein one of South Africa's Billionaires was showing me where he hid his treasures. His treasures consisted of gold and silver bars, diamonds and many other precious stones and metals. I will talk more on this in chapter nine.

Chapter Six

Cyrus- Strengthened by God

"Thus saith the LORD to his anointed, to Cyrus, whose right hand I have holden, to subdue nations before him; and I will loose the loins of kings, to open before him the two leaved gates; and the gates shall not be shut; I will go before thee, and make the crooked places straight: I will break in pieces the gates of brass, and cut in sunder the bars of iron: And I will give thee the treasures of darkness, and hidden riches of secret places, that thou mayest know that, the LORD, which call thee by thy name, am the God of Israel. For Jacob my servant's sake, and Israel mine elect, I have even called thee by thy name: I have surnamed thee, though thou hast not known me. I am the LORD, and there is none else, there is no God beside me: I girded thee, though thou hast not known me: That they may know from the rising of the sun, and from the west, that there is none beside me. I am the LORD, and there is none else" **(Isaiah 45v1-6).**

Chapter five of this book dealt with and focused largely on the "anointing" aspect of Cyrus. In this chapter we will look at the "Right Hand of Cyrus" or that which the Cyrus Anointing enabled King Cyrus to accomplish. This we will do by gleaning on the other aspects that are locked up in our above scriptural study text.

Right Hand

One of the things that God points out in Isaiah 45v1 is that He is holding the right hand of King Cyrus. In other words, God Almighty has strengthened and empowered King Cyrus's right hand. This tells us that king Cyrus was not operating with his own human power and strength. He wasn't even merely operating from his royal authority. King Cyrus operated under the strength and power of Almighty God.

It is important to remember that the right hand is a hand of the firstborn blessing. It is a hand of power and generally the strongest hand for most human beings. The right hand is also the hand of a cunning skilled warrior. The right hand is a hand that saves. The right hand also executes judgment.

Our Lord and Saviour Jesus Christ of Nazareth, when He rose from the dead and before He ascended to heaven said; *"....., All power is given unto me in heaven and in earth." (**Matthew 28v18**).* The Bible also teaches us that Jesus Christ is seated on the right hand of God. **(Mark 16v19).** Because *"all power is given unto me in heaven and in earth",* Jesus Christ sits on the right hand of the Father.

Hand of the Firstborn Blessing

When Jacob wanted to bless the children of Joseph, he crossed his hands and put his right hand on the head of Ephraim (the youngest) and his left hand on Manasseh (the firstborn). Once, Joseph realised this, he protested that Jacob had placed his right hand on the younger of the two brothers.

Jacob responded and said he was well aware of that and he wasn't making a mistake. He continued to tell Joseph that though Manasseh would also be great, the reality was that Ephraim, the younger brother would be greater than Manasseh. Joseph protested because he understood that the right hand is the hand of the blessing of the firstborn and under normal circumstances, Manasseh was entitled to that blessing.

The favour and blessing of God upon those called and endued with the Cyrus Anointing, will not be ordinary but extraordinary. It will be a logic defying and tradition breaking type of favour and blessing. They may have been despised and looked down upon by the people but when the Cyrus Anointing shows up in their lives, they will be promoted and elevated to places they never thought possible.

Because God Almighty holds their right hand, they will be accelerated in every single thing that they do. What takes others ten years to achieve they will be able to achieve overnight. There will be so much grace upon their lives to an extent that, the wealth that took others a lifetime to amass, it will take them only a year. They will be like a runner that comes from the back and outruns everyone else to win the race.

I want to point out though that this will all be dependent on their willingness to walk with God. It will be dependent on their ability to step out in faith and obey God. It will also be dependent on their ability to listen to the guiding voice of the Holy Spirit.

The blessing of the firstborn is not a normal blessing. It always goes much further and beyond what is ordinary. Think about what people consider to be blessed. Have you got a picture of that in mind? Now, go far beyond that and exceed it in an immeasurable manner. The blessing of the firstborn is God doing exceedingly, abundantly, immeasurably more that anyone can think, ask or imagine, according to His power that is at work within His anointed ones.

Hand of Power

> *"Thy right hand, O LORD, is become glorious in power: thy right hand, O LORD, hath dashed in pieces the enemy."* ***(Exodus 15v6)***

> *"Thou stretchedst out thy right hand, the earth swallowed them."* ***(Exodus 15v12)***

The right hand is the hand of power. Power is the ability to change circumstances and conditions for the better. When Israel was attacked by the enemy, the right hand of the LORD dashed their enemy to pieces. When the right hand of the LORD was stretched against the enemies of Israel, the earth opened up and swallowed the enemies of Israel.

Because, God held King Cyrus's right hand, the enemies of King Cyrus did not even stand a chance against him. King Cyrus conquered all his enemies without much of an effort. That is because; he wasn't fighting by his own strength.

As they tap into and walk in the fullness of the Cyrus Anointing, they will be mighty in spiritual warfare. Remember that New Testament believers endued with the Cyrus Anointing, do not war against flesh and blood. Their warfare is against principalities, powers, rulers of the darkness of this world and against spiritual wickedness in high places. **(Ephesians 6v12)**

When walking in the Cyrus Anointing, God will assign them to confront ancient territorial devils. These are devils that have set themselves over nations, regions, cities and even the different sectors of the economy. These are principalities that have established themselves as rulers within these spheres. The Cyrus Anointing will confront, engage in warfare with and dislodge these principalities. In so doing, the Cyrus Anointing will establish the reign of Jesus Christ our Lord and Saviour in all these domains.

Hand of Skill

> *"If I forget thee, O Jerusalem, let my right hand forget her cunning."* ***(Psalm 137v5)***

> *"If I forget you, O Jerusalem, may my right hand forget [its skill]."* ***(Psalm 137v5 NIV)***

The right hand is a hand of skill. It is a hand of competence, precision, accuracy and mastery. This therefore means that King Cyrus was highly skilled. He handled his assignment with skill, competence, precision, accuracy and mastery.

Those that are called to walk in the Cyrus Anointing will exhibit skill, competence, precision, accuracy and mastery that are far beyond average. There is no substitute for excellence for those that are called to walk in the Cyrus Anointing.

It is for this reason that I want to encourage everyone that identifies with the Cyrus Anointing to polish their skills and gifting and remain abreast of developments in their sphere of Godly assignment (media, finance, business, politics, academia etc). In reality, those who are called and anointed to walk in the Cyrus Anointing are not just to be abreast of developments but to pioneer these developments. They are to be the ones introducing new trends and developments.

Hand of Judgment

> *"Then Jael Heber's wife took a nail of the tent, and took an hammer in her hand, and went softly unto him, and smote the nail into his temples, and fastened it into the ground: for he was fast asleep and weary. So he died."* ***(Judges 4v21)***

> *"She put her hand to the nail, and her right hand to the workmen's hammer; and with the hammer she smote Sisera, she smote off his head, when she had pierced and stricken through his temples."* ***(Judges 5v26)***

The right hand is the hand that executes judgment against the enemies of God. King Cyrus was called, chosen and anointed by God Almighty to carry out the judgment of God upon Babylon. This judgment was because Babylon exceeded the measure of judgment that God had intended for Babylon to inflict on the nation of Israel. Through the mouth of Isaiah the Prophet God tells Babylon that;

> *"I was wroth with my people, I have polluted mine inheritance, and given them into thine hand: thou didst shew them no mercy; upon the ancient hast thou very heavily laid thy yoke"* **(Isaiah 47:6)**.

Babylon went above and beyond the punishment that God wanted them to inflict on Israel. It is because of this that God had to strengthen King Cyrus's right hand in punishing Babylon.

Those endued with the Cyrus Anointing will be able to pronounce the judgment of the LORD. They will exercise judgment over situations and give the counsel of the LORD. They will also be able to pronounce judgment over all the enemies of God in the earth.

Unlike Jael, Heber's wife that is quoted in the above two scriptures above. The Cyrus Anointing will not execute judgment by physically executing people but they will rather pronounce words of judgment against the enemies of God. This sort of judgment will be in the same manner that Jesus Christ spoke to the tree and it dried up from the roots. It will be the kind of judgment that is like Paul speaking to Elymas and Elymas instantaneously becoming blind. This judgment will be spoken against those individuals and groupings that are enemies of the will of God in the earth.

Hand of Salvation

> *"Shew thy marvellous loving kindness, O thou that savest by thy right hand them which put their trust in thee from those that rise up against them."* **(Psalm 17v7)**

> *"Now know I that the LORD saveth his anointed; he will hear him from his holy heaven with the saving strength of his right hand."* **(Psalm 20v6)**

The right hand is the hand of salvation. It is a hand that saves. It is a hand that delivers and rescues those that are in danger. That is why those that are endued with the Cyrus Anointing will be a people that win souls. They will be engaged in mass evangelism by means of funding the evangelistic crusades and partnering with evangelists and other ministers that are reaching the lost with the Gospel of Jesus Christ.

Not only that. The Cyrus Anointing will rescue and deliver many from different types of bondages including financial bondages. So many people are trapped in debt. As a result of that they have no peace and are therefore unable to serve the LORD. They are serving their creditors. The Cyrus Anointing will free people from the shackles of debt.

Hand of Victory

> *"O sing unto the LORD a new song; for he hath done marvellous things: his right hand, and his holy arm, hath gotten him the victory."* **(Psalm 98v1)**

> *"The voice of rejoicing and salvation is in the tabernacles of the righteous: the right hand of the LORD doeth valiantly. The right hand of the LORD is exalted: the right hand of the LORD doeth valiantly."*
> ***(Psalm 116v15-16)***

Victory is brought about by the right hand. Mighty things are the product of the right hand. Those who are called to walk in the Cyrus Anointing will experience victory in each of the assignments, mandates and tasks given to them by the LORD God Almighty. That is why it is critical for them to be absolutely sure that whatever they expend energy on is something that God instructed them to do.

Lastly, as we have seen above, the right hand is the hand of; the firstborn blessing, power, skill, victory, salvation and judgment. However, all of these did not come solely as a result of King Cyrus's ability. His (Cyrus) right hand was strengthened by God Almighty. God Almighty enabled King Cyrus to; be a blessing, administer salvation and judgment, walk in power and victory, and exhibit incomparable skills.

It is for this reason that those who are called to walk in the Cyrus Anointing should resist the temptation to trust in their own strength, learning and knowledge. The reason for this is because that which they are called to accomplish is far greater than their own abilities can accomplish. It is also because it is not by might nor by power but by the Spirit of God that they can accomplish their assignments.

Because of this, those who are called to walk in the Cyrus Anointing today are to be completely dependent on the strength and ability of God. The fact that God says He's holding Cyrus's right hand indicates that, on its own, Cyrus's right hand is completely weak and incapable of accomplishing this great assignment and mandate. It is in this state of weakness that the strength of God will show up. Remember what the LORD said to apostle Paul; *"......,My grace is sufficient for thee: for my strength is made perfect in weakness"* ***(2 Corinthians 12:9).***

If they try to rely on their own knowledge, strength and learning; they will dilute and contaminate that which God wants to do through them. That is why it becomes increasingly critical that they don't involve the flesh in that which God is doing. Instead they should allow the grace of God within them to work through them. Remember, apostle Paul says; *"......; but I laboured more abundantly than they all: yet not I, but the grace of God which was with me"* ***(1 Corinthians 15:10).*** They must allow God to hold and strengthen their right hand.

Chapter Seven

Subduing Nations

"Thus saith the LORD to his anointed, to Cyrus, whose right hand I have holden, to subdue nations before him; and I will loose the loins of kings, to open before him the two leaved gates; and the gates shall not be shut; I will go before thee, and make the crooked places straight: I will break in pieces the gates of brass, and cut in sunder the bars of iron: And I will give thee the treasures of darkness, and hidden riches of secret places, that thou mayest know that, the LORD, which call thee by thy name, am the God of Israel. For Jacob my servant's sake, and Israel mine elect, I have even called thee by thy name: I have surnamed thee, though thou hast not known me. I am the LORD, and there is none else, there is no God beside me: I girded thee, though thou hast not known me: That they may know from the rising of the sun, and from the west, that there is none beside me. I am the LORD, and there is none else" **(Isaiah 45v1-6).**

One of the key things that God promised to do through King Cyrus is that King Cyrus would subdue nations. This means that Cyrus is given authority to rule over not just one nation but nations. The sphere of influence and dominance that was given to King Cyrus was not only local, trans-local, continental but a global sphere of dominance, influence and rulership.

Even though there is not much recorded in the Bible about the conquest and dominance of King Cyrus over many other nations besides Babylon, there is several passages of scripture that give us a detailed prophetic indication of the conquest and dominance of King Cyrus. One such prophetic indication is found in the book of Daniel where the Bible says;

> *"Then I lifted up mine eyes, and saw, and, behold, there stood before the river a ram which had two horns; and the two horns were high; but one was higher than the other, and the higher came up last. I saw the ram pushing westward, and northward, and southward; so that no beast might stand before him, neither was there any that could deliver out of his hand; but he did according to his will, and became great.....The ram which thou sawest having two horns are the kings of Media and Persia"* ***(Daniel 8:3-4,20).***

The above prophetic vision that Daniel saw is about the kingdom of the Medes and Persians. The ram represents the kings of Media and Persia. As stated in Daniel chapter eight, the longer horn which came up last, represents King Cyrus. It is very clear from this vision that the kingdom of the Medes and Persians was a world super power that gained this world super power status and prominence under King Cyrus as it pushed westward, and northward and southward. It is made very clear in both Isaiah 41 verse 2 and 46 verse 11 that King Cyrus was from the East.

To subdue means to bring under the control and dominance of the other. This is done by force. It is not voluntary. Before one can subdue a nation or nations, one must firstly conquer the one to be subdued in the battlefield. You must conquer them to the point of them having no other option but to surrender and submit under your leadership, authority and governance.

Alongside the historical evidence, there is very clear scriptural prophetic evidence that indicates that King Cyrus would subdue, conquer and dominate many nations. This scriptural prophetic evidence is found in several places in the Bible including our basic study text in Isaiah 45:2. The other scriptural prophetic evidence is found in Isaiah 41 and it says;

> *"Who raised up the righteous man from the east, called him to his foot, <u>gave the nations before him, and made him rule over kings? He gave them as dust to his sword, and as driven stubble to his bow.</u> He pursued them, and passed safely; even by the way that he had not gone with his feet...I have raised up one from the north, and he shall come: from the rising of the sun shall he call upon my name: <u>and he shall come upon princes as upon morter, and as the potter treadeth clay"</u> **(Isaiah 41:2-3,25).***

The vision of Daniel states that the ram pushed westward, northward and southward. The fact that the ram was pushing westward, northward and southward makes it very clear that the pushing was from the east side. It is my conclusion that the ram must have already conquered, subdued and consolidated the East before starting to push westward, northward and southward to conquer and subdue the four corners of the earth.

It is very clear in the book of Isaiah forty one and verse two that God gave the nations before King Cyrus and also made him rule over kings. God gave the nations and kings as dust to the sword of King Cyrus and as driven stubble to his bow. The Contemporary English Version of the Bible says; *"....His sword and his arrows turn them to dust blown by the wind."* The dust that kings and nations are turned to by the sword and arrows of King Cyrus is the same dust that God spoke about in Genesis 3:19 when He told Adam that *"....for dust thou art, and unto dust shalt thou return."*

Actually, besides the scriptural prophetic evidence that King Cyrus would conquer, subdue and dominate many nations, there is a scriptural and historical record that King Cyrus did indeed conquer, subdue and rule over all the nations of the earth. In the Cyrus Decree that King Cyrus issued in the books of Ezra chapter one and Second Chronicles thirty six, King Cyrus announced that Almighty God had given him all the kingdoms of the earth. The Bible says;

> *"Thus saith Cyrus king of Persia, All the kingdoms of the earth hath the LORD God of heaven given me;...."* ***(2 Chronicles 36:23).***

> *"This is what Cyrus king of Persia says: "The LORD, the God of heaven, has given me all the kingdoms of the earth..."* ***(2 Chronicles 36:23 NIV).***

> *"This is what king Cyrus of Persia says: "The LORD, the God of heaven, has given me all the kingdoms of the earth"* ***(2 Chronicles 36:23 NLT).***

> *"The message said: "I am King Cyrus of Persia. The LORD God of heaven has made me the ruler of every nation on earth"*** (2 Chronicles 36:23 CEV).***

It is very clear and evident from the above various translations of second chronicles thirty six and twenty three that God gave King Cyrus rulership and dominion over all the kingdoms and nations of the earth and not just some of them. The book of Ezra in chapter one, also confirms that King Cyrus was given world domination by Almighty God.

The Cyrus Anointing being released from heaven today carries the same mandate. It will conquer the forces of darkness. It will break the stubborn evil princes that rule and govern over the nations on the surface of the earth. This will be done by means of spiritual warfare. After conquering the evil princes that rule over the nations, those carrying the Cyrus Anointing will be able to win that nation to the Lordship of Jesus Christ. This will be the fulfilment of the Great Commission that our Lord Jesus Christ has given to the Church and it says;

> *"And Jesus came and spake unto them, saying, All power is given unto me in heaven and in earth. Go ye therefore, and teach all nations, baptizing them in the name of the Father, and of the Son, and of the Holy Ghost: Teaching them to observe all things whatsoever I have commanded you: and, lo, I am with*

you always, even unto the end of the world. Amen" (Matthew 28:18-20).

Those walking in the Cyrus Anointing will find immeasurable favour within the nations they subdue. They will be able to speak to the presidents of nations. They will even be requested to serve as special presidential advisers. The arrogance and stubbornness of many nations will be broken. The Cyrus Anointing is an anointing of global; impact, influence and dominion.

Those called and anointed with the Cyrus Anointing will be global and international business man and women and statesmen and women. They will be global practitioners and pioneers in the various fields and spheres of their God-given assignment such as politics, law, economics, business, sport, entertainment, Science & Technology, Education and many others. They will be global specialists that are in demand among all the nations of the earth. They will be global investors. Their footprint will be global.

It is because of this grace and anointing for global impact, influence and dominion that the Cyrus Anointing will accelerate the fulfilment of the Great Commission. This is because, much like ancient Babylon, all the nations of the earth will be favourably disposed to those that walk in the Cyrus Anointing. The full and unlimited release of the Cyrus Anointing will bring the Church to the place of fulfilling Acts 3:21 as well as the fulfilment of Revelations 11:15.

Chapter Eight

Stripping the Armour of Kings

"Thus saith the LORD to his anointed, to Cyrus, whose right hand I have holden, to subdue nations before him; and I will loose the loins of kings, to open before him the two leaved gates; and the gates shall not be shut; I will go before thee, and make the crooked places straight: I will break in pieces the gates of brass, and cut in sunder the bars of iron: And I will give thee the treasures of darkness, and hidden riches of secret places, that thou mayest know that, the LORD, which call thee by thy name, am the God of Israel. For Jacob my servant's sake, and Israel mine elect, I have even called thee by thy name: I have surnamed thee, though thou hast not known me. I am the LORD, and there is none else, there is no God beside me: I girded thee, though thou hast not known me: That they may know from the rising of the sun, and from the west, that there is none beside me. I am the LORD, and there is none else" **(Isaiah 45v1-6).**

God promises to loose the loins of kings or strip the kings off their armour before King Cyrus. The NIV version of the Bible says; *"....and to strip kings of their armour,..."*. Loins are symbolic representations of both the armour and reproductive seed. They represent both the physical strength in armoury as well as the strength that is found in one's children. Remember the Bible says; *"Children are like arrows in the hand of a mighty man. Blessed is the man whose quiver is full of them (paraphrase).* It is on the loins that men wear their armour. When one's armour is stripped from them, they are weakened and vulnerable in the battle without their armour.

The NLT version of the Bible says; *"....mighty kings will be paralyzed with fear".* When King Cyrus was on the way to attack Babylon, the Bible records that the king of Babylon was so afraid to an extent that his hands hung limp in despair and hopelessness. The Bible says;

> *"The king of Babylon hath heard the report of them, and his hands waxed feeble: anguish took hold of him, and pangs as of a woman in travail." **(Jeremiah 50v43)***

> *"The king of Babylon has heard reports about them, and his hands hang limp. Anguish has gripped him, pain like that of a woman in labour." **(Jeremiah 50v43 NIV)***

> *"The king of Babylon has heard reports about the enemy, and he is weak with fright. Pangs of anguish have gripped him, like those of a woman in labor." **(Jeremiah 50v43 NLT)***

> *"Babylon's king hears them coming. He goes white as a ghost, limp as a dishrag. Terror-stricken, he doubles up in pain, helpless to fight, like a woman*

*giving birth to a baby." **(Jeremiah 50v43 The Message)***

The state of affairs outlined and foretold in Jeremiah 50 verse 43 is actually fulfilled and plays out in the book of Daniel. The Bible tells us about a time wherein Belshazzar, the son of king Nebuchadnezzar was now reigning as king. In the account of Daniel chapter five, the Bible tells us that King Belshazzar gave an instruction to bring out the sacred silver and gold vessels that his father Nebuchadnezzar had taken from the temple of God in Jerusalem.

His reason for calling for these vessels was so that, both he and his nobles, officials and concubines could drink wine from these vessels. They did not just drink wine from them but as they were drinking wine from the sacred vessels, they praised the gods of gold, silver and brass. It is at this point that the disembodied hand appeared and wrote on the wall. The Bible tells us that;

> "In the same hour came forth fingers of a man's hand, and wrote over against the candlestick upon the plaster of the wall of the king's palace: and the king saw the part of the hand that wrote. <u>Then the king's countenance was changed, and his thoughts troubled him, so that the joints of his loins were loosed, and his knees smote one against another</u>" **(Daniel 5:5-6)**.

King Belshazzar was so scared so much that his knees were clapping. The New Living Translation says that; "his legs gave way beneath him". Belshazzar was so overcome with fear so much that he could not stand on his own two feet. His legs experienced sudden paralysis. This paralysis came as a result of the hand appearing and writing on the wall. This is how God loosed the loins of the king of Babylon before King Cyrus.

What made matters worse for the king of Babylon is the fact that none of his wise men, astrologers, diviners and enchanters could read what was written on the wall. Eventually, the king's mother advised him that there was a man named Daniel who had the Spirit of God in him and to whom no mystery was too great or complicated. They called Daniel in and Daniel gave them the interpretation. The interpretation was that God had pronounced eminent judgment upon Babylon.

Now, the reason why God loosed the loins of kings before King Cyrus was so that, those kings could open the gates in surrender before King Cyrus. Ancient cities had walls and gates in them. The gates were meant to keep the unwanted outside of the city. There was even access control at the city gates. There were men that were assigned to screen those that came into the city.

King Cyrus wasn't restricted in his movements. He had free reign and free access into the cities as the kings he subdued opened the gates for him at will. This was because the terror of the LORD was upon the kings and they were terrified of King Cyrus. The open gates gave King Cyrus access to all the resources within the city protected by the gates. Jeremiah the prophet tells us the following about Babylon;

"Shout against her round about: <u>she hath given her hand</u>: her foundations are fallen, her walls are thrown down: for it is the vengeance of the LORD: take vengeance upon her; as she hath done, do unto her" ***(Jeremiah 50:15).***

"Shout against her on every side! <u>She surrenders</u>, her towers fall, her walls are torn down. Since this is the vengeance of the LORD, take vengeance on her; do to her as she has done to others" ***(Jeremiah 50:15 NIV).***

"Shout war cries against her from every side. <u>Look! She surrenders</u>! Her walls have fallen. It is the LORD's vengeance, so take vengeance on her. Do to her as she has done to others" ***(Jeremiah 50:15 NLT).***

"Shout battle cries from every direction. <u>All the fight has gone out of her</u>. Her defences have been flattened, her walls smashed. 'Operation GOD's Vengeance.' Pile on the vengeance! Do to her as she has done. Give her a good dose of her own medicine!" ***(Jeremiah 50:15 The Message).***

The terror of God fell upon Babylon and every other nation that King Cyrus and his army were coming to attack. These nations and their kings were brought to a state of complete fear and paralysis by the news and report that King Cyrus and his army were coming to attack them. Because of the terror of the presence of God that went before King Cyrus, these nations literally surrendered and did not mount up a fight against King Cyrus and his army. The Bible tells us that;

> *"The mighty men of Babylon have forborn to fight, they have remained in their holds: their might hath failed; they became as women:......"* ***(Jeremiah 51:30).***

> *"Babylon's warriors have stopped fighting; they remain in their strongholds. Their strength is exhausted; they have become weaklings"* ***(Jeremiah 51:30 NIV).***

> *"Her mightiest warriors no longer fight. They stay in their barracks, their courage gone. They have become like women"* ***(Jeremiah 51:30 NLT)***

> *"Babylon's soldiers have quit fighting. They hide out in ruins and caves – Cowards who've given up without a fight, exposed as cowering milksops"* ***(Jeremiah 51:30 The Message).***

This is a very vivid picture of the manner in which God stripped the armour of kings before King Cyrus. This verse reveals to us that the soldiers of Babylon were gripped by a spirit of fear to an extent that they hid themselves away from King Cyrus and his army. This means that, the soldiers that were supposed to be guarding the gates of the city and doing access control actually abandoned their posts. They absconded and left the gates of the city of Babylon unattended.

As God promised that; *"......;.. the gates shall not be shut"*, the gates of Babylon were indeed not shut. Instead they were abandoned by the soldiers that were meant to protect them. This state of abandoned gates provided King Cyrus and his army with unlimited access to the city of Babylon as well as all its resources and infrastructure.

One of the key things that God promised King Cyrus by the mouth of Isaiah the Prophet is that; *"I will go before thee, and make crooked places straight: I will break in pieces the gates of brass, and cut in sunder the bars of iron:"*. Indeed, God Almighty went before King Cyrus and made the crooked places straight.

God did this levelling of mountains and straightening of paths before King Cyrus by causing the fingers of a man's hand to write on the wall the judgment that God had pronounced against Babylon. The appearing of this hand caused all of Babylon to be extremely frightened. The interpretation that Daniel gave made the crooked places straight and broke in pieces the gates of brass. This cleared the obstacles for King Cyrus and his army. The interpretation that Daniel gave was, *"MENE; God hath numbered thy kingdom, and finished it. TEKEL; Thou art weight in the balances, and art found wanting. PERES; Thy kingdom is divided, and given to the Medes and Persians"* **(Daniel 5:26-28).**

It will be no different for those whom God has called and is raising to walk in the Cyrus Anointing today. God will loose the loins of kings before this breed of believers. He will cause His terror to fall upon both the evil principalities manipulating regions and cities; and upon those that are opposed to the will and counsel of God in the earth but occupy key leadership positions in all sectors of the economy.

The Cyrus Anointing is not subject to restrictions. Both satanic and unjust manmade restrictions that are designed to keep people out of certain sectors of the economy or governance will not be closed to those anointed with the Cyrus Anointing. They are given free reign and free access to go into the gates and possess the precious things of the enemy.

This free reign that is afforded to those that walk in the Cyrus Anointing means that the carriers of the Cyrus Anointing need to be very responsible and walk circumspectly. The fact that there are no restrictions means that one can easily go rogue and misuse their God-given authority. That is why the Cyrus Anointing requires a high level of maturity.

Without this maturity, some will not be able to handle the kind of power and authority in the Cyrus Anointing. The lives of those anointed with the Cyrus Anointing must be fully submitted to God Almighty and under the Lordship of Jesus Christ. The fear of the LORD must be their treasure and their guiding principle. In that way, they will be able to maintain the course and not fall into the trap of the devil.

The open gates will usher them to wealth and resources. These gates will usher them to influence over large numbers of people. Many will trust them with their lives and their most precious things. That is why the fear of the LORD needs to become their guiding principle. They need to live their lives before God Almighty in full submission and accountability to His Word.

As they go about executing the mandate and assignment that God has given them, God will cause their enemies to hear about them before they even get to them. Territorial devils will hear about them as they are coming into their region and sphere of influence long before they even get there. This reminds me of a vision I had many years back around the year 2001.

I was leading an apostolic and prophetic team from my home Church. It was a team of two men (including me) and three women. We were sent by the senior pastor of our congregation to visit a sister congregation in Mdantsane - East London, South Africa. East London is a three hour drive from Port Elizabeth (my home town).

We left Port Elizabeth around 6 in the morning and we were meant to be in East London and strengthen the sister congregation for a week. On arrival, I decided to take a nap. I wasn't even sleeping when I began to see mummies falling from the sky. In fact, they seemed to be falling from the street light poles. They were wrapped like the mummies of ancient Egypt. They kept on dropping to the ground.

On seeing that, I then realized that God had already given us victory in the work that we had come to do. This was evident as the demonic entities that were influencing and manipulating that place were beginning to fall long before we even commenced with the work we had come to do. The demonic entities in that place recognised that greater power and authority had come into the region. They recognized the greater One in us, Jesus Christ the Son of the Living God.

These evil spirits will recognize them just like the demon that spoke through the demon possessed man to the sons of Sceva and said; *"......Jesus I know, and Paul I know; but who are ye?" (Acts 19v15).* Evil spirits recognize spiritual ranking. They recognize higher ranking. They will recognize them too because; *"......greater is he that is in you, than he that is in the world." (1 John 4v4).*

The terror of the LORD will be on their enemies and they will fear them. This will not be because of their doing. It will not be because of their own might or strength. It will be because they will be busy executing the will and counsel of the LORD.

Lastly, God will cause kings to be favourably disposed to those that are called and anointed with the Cyrus Anointing. This will be a state of surrender just like the state of Babylon that is mentioned above as found in Jeremiah 50:15. God will turn the hearts of kings towards those anointed with the Cyrus Anointing. Remember the Bible says; *"In the LORD's hand the king's heart is a stream of water that he channels toward all who please him"* ***(Proverbs 21:1 NIV).***

Chapter Nine

Treasures of Darkness and Hidden Riches of Secret Places

> *"And I will give thee the treasures of darkness, and hidden riches of secret places, that thou mayest know that, the LORD, which call thee by thy name, am the God of Israel. For Jacob my servant's sake, and Israel mine elect, I have even called thee by thy name: I have surnamed thee, though thou hast not known me. I am the LORD, and there is none else, there is no God beside me: I girded thee, though thou hast not known me: That they may know from the rising of the sun, and from the west, that there is none beside me. I am the LORD, and there is none else"* **(Isaiah 45v1-6).**

One of the key promises that God made to King Cyrus was that of **giving** him the treasures of darkness and hidden riches of secret places. So determined and committed was God to giving King Cyrus the treasures of darkness and hidden riches of secret places to an extent that God undertook to; 1. Strip kings off their armour, 2. Go before King Cyrus, 3. Make crooked places straight for King Cyrus, 4. Break in pieces gates of brass and cut in sunder bars of iron before King Cyrus.

In the previous chapter we did an extensive look at God stripping kings off their armour before King Cyrus. At this point I want us to take a look at other critical aspects outlined above before we look at God giving the treasures of darkness and hidden riches of secret places to King Cyrus. We will, obviously, as we have done in all the other chapters have a look at the meaning and application for those who are called and anointed to walk in the Cyrus Anointing today.

I Will Go Before Thee

> *"I will go before thee, and make the crooked places straight: I will break in pieces the gates of brass, and cut in sunder the bars of iron."* ***(Isaiah 45v2)***

As if all that which God did for Cyrus in verse one of Isaiah forty five wasn't enough, God promises to go before King Cyrus. This speaks of God leading King Cyrus into victory every step of the way. It was impossible for King Cyrus to lose because he walked in the footsteps of God Almighty. This is evidenced by what God says through Isaiah the Prophet when He says;

> *"....., and I will direct all his ways:.."* ***(Isaiah 45:13).***
>
> *"...., and I will guide his actions"* ***(Isaiah 45:13 NLT).***

It is clearly evident from the above scripture quotation that God Almighty was directing and guiding all of King Cyrus's ways and actions. This is simply because King Cyrus was especially chosen by God for a unique and precious assignment from God. That unique and precious assignment from God was the destruction of Babylon and the freeing of the people of Israel, God's inheritance, from Babylonian slavery and subjugation.

It is because God Almighty had a vested interest in the destruction of Babylon and the liberation of the Israelites from Babylonian captivity. This is why God had to get personally involved in the settling of the score with Babylon. Remember that the Bible says of Israel that Israel is the apple of God's eye. This is why God took a personal interest in the destruction of Babylon.

The other thing that God promises He will do as He goes before King Cyrus is to *"make the crooked places straight"*. The New International Version of the Bible reads as *".....and will level mountains;"*. The mountains had no choice but to be levelled before God Almighty. Remember that the Bible says the following;

> *"The mountains melt like wax before the LORD, before the Lord of all the earth"* **(Psalm 97:5 NIV).**

God going before King Cyrus yielded the result of mountains melting before God. The mountains melted before God because they were terrified and paralyzed at the sight of God Almighty. Obviously this is not literally. I am not saying that mountains cannot literally melt before the LORD. In fact I am of the view that mountains can and do literally melt before God.

You may be asking how an inanimate object such as a mountain can respond to God? It is critical that we don't forget that all creation is subject to Almighty God. As a matter of fact there is scriptural evidence of an inanimate object responding and bowing to God Almighty. Remember the god of the Philistines? The Bible tells us that Dagon the god (an inanimate object) of the Philistines bowed and lay prostrate before God.

This is the advantage of the Cyrus Anointing. God Almighty Himself goes before those He has called and anointed with the Cyrus Anointing. He leads them in the way that they should go. As God goes before them, He makes the crooked places straight. God Almighty levels the mountains and exalts the valleys before them. When the Cyrus Anointing is assigned by God to go and goes into any city, region or nation; that city, region, nation or sector of the economy will have heard about the anointing that is coming their way. All obstacles will have been removed by the LORD God Almighty Himself.

All spiritual gates (evil princes and entities) of brass and spiritual bars of iron that will want to keep the Cyrus Anointing out of a city, region, nation or economic sector will be broken to pieces by Jehovah God. These are all the evil entities that sit upon many waters (multitudes) to oppress, manipulate and control them. They will be broken in the same manner that Samson broke and carried away to the top of a hill the city gates of Gaza. **(Judges 16v1-3)**

Because of this, those that are anointed with the Cyrus Anointing will experience inexplicable, extreme and immeasurable favour. They will experience and witness this inexplicable, extreme, immeasurable and unfathomable favour in ministry, business, politics, academia, finance, and all the other sectors of society.

Treasures of Darkness and Hidden Riches of Secret Places

When Nebuchadnezzar the king of Babylon overthrew Jerusalem, there are some treasures and riches that he took and carried away into Babylon. These were spoils of war that belonged to the victor (which in this case was Nebuchadnezzar). The book of 2 Kings 24-25 catalogues those treasures and riches that the king of Babylon took away. We also mentioned that Nebuchadnezzar carried away the vessels of the temple of God.

When looking at what God meant when He promised to give treasures of darkness and hidden riches of secret places to King Cyrus, it is important to remember that Babylon and its king was used by God to inflict judgment on other nations too, not just Israel. These are the nations that were also enemies of Israel. Now, let us look at what the Bible says;

> *"In the beginning of the reign of Jehoiakim the son of Josiah king of Judah came this word unto Jeremiah from the LORD, saying, Thus saith the LORD to me; Make thee bonds and yokes, and put them upon thy neck, And send them to the king of Edom, and to the king of Moab, and to the king of the Ammonites, and to the king of Tyrus, and to the king Zidon, by the hand of the messengers which come to Jerusalem unto Zedekiah king of Judah; And command them to say*

unto their masters, Thus saith the LORD of hosts, the God of Israel; Thus shall ye say unto your masters; I have made the earth, the man and the beast that are upon the ground, by my great power and by my outstretched arm, and have given it unto whom it seemed meet unto me. And now have I given all these lands into the hand of Nebuchadnezzar the king of Babylon, my servant; and the beasts of the field have I given him also to serve him. And all nations shall serve him, and his son, and his son's son, until the very time of his land come: and then many nations and great kings shall serve themselves of him. And it shall come to pass, that the nation and kingdom which will not serve the same Nebuchadnezzar king of Babylon, and that will not put their neck under the yoke of the king of Babylon, that nation will I punish, saith the LORD, with the sword, and with the famine, and with the pestilence, until I have consumed them by his hand." (Jeremiah 27v1-8)

We can clearly see from the above scripture quotation that there were several other nations that were conquered and subdued by Nebuchadnezzar the king of Babylon. Raiding the defeated nations and taking away their treasures and hidden riches was a common practise in those days. Those who returned from the battle, returned with the spoils of war.

Nebuchadnezzar also retuned with the gold, silver and other precious things from the nations he conquered. He emptied the treasuries and reserves of the nations that he defeated. It is not only the national wealth of those nations that got dispossessed by the king of Babylon but the wealth of their citizens. All the wealth that belonged to their great men and women.

The wealth, treasures and riches that Nebuchadnezzar took from all the nations that he defeated served merely as a surplus to the existing wealth of Babylon. As a result of that, it was not used. It merely got stored up in secret places of darkness. Remember, the Bible says of Babylon; *"O thou that dwellest upon many waters, abundant in treasures, thine end is come, and the measure of thy covetousness."* **(Jeremiah 51v13).** This wealth was stored up so that it can advance the agenda and sustain the rule of Babylon through the descendants of the king of Babylon.

There are several Bible commentators that shed some light into how the treasures and riches that King Nebuchadnezzar had pillaged from all the nations he defeated were hidden and stored. At this point, I want to take a look at and quote a few Bible commentaries that are shedding some light into the hiding and storing of these treasures and riches.

The **Jamieson-Fausset-Brown Bible Commentary** states the following;

> *"Treasures of darkness – that is, hidden in subterranean places; a common Oriental practice. Sorcerers pretended to be able to show where such treasures were to be found; in opposition to their pretensions, God says, He will really give hidden treasures to Cyrus (Jer 50:37; 51:13). Pliny (Natural History, 33:3) says that Cyrus obtained from the*

> *conquest of Asia thirty-four thousand pounds weight of gold, besides golden vases, and five hundred thousand talents of silver, and the goblet of Semiramis, weighing fifteen talents."*

Gill's Exposition of the Entire Bible on the other hand says the following;

> *"And I will give thee treasures of darkness, and hidden riches of secret places,.....What had been laid up in private places, and had not seen the light for many years. The Jewish Rabbins say (f), that Nebuchadnezzar having amassed together all the riches of the world, when he drew near his end, considered with himself to whom he should leave it; and being unwilling to leave it to Evilmerodach, he ordered ships of brass to be built, and filled them with it, and dug a place in Euphrates, and hid them in it, and turned the river upon them; and that day that Cyrus ordered the temple to be built, the Lord revealed them to him: the riches of Croesus king of Lydia, taken by Cyrus, are meant; especially what he found in Babylon, which abounded in riches, Jeremiah 51:13. Piny (g) says, when he conquered Asia, he brought away thirty four thousand pounds of gold, besides golden vessels, and five hundred thousand talents of silver, and the cup of Semiramis, which weighed fifteen talents. Xenophon (h) makes mention of great riches and treasures which Cyrus received from Armenius, Gobryas, and Croesus:"*

The **Cambridge Bible for Schools and Colleges** states the following;

> *"**the treasures of dakness**]* i.e. treasures hid in darkness. The following word rendered **hidden riches** (Heb. **matmon**, held by some to be the original of the N.T. "Mammon"), means properly treasure **hidden underground** (Job 3:21; Proverbs 2:4; Jeremiah 41:8). The treasures referred to are chiefly the loot of Sardis, which Xenophon describes as "the richest city of Asia next to Babylon" (Cyrop. VII. 2. 11), and of Babylon itself (Jeremiah 50:37; Jeremiah 51:13). If, as a probable, the capture of the former city was past before the date of the prophecy, rumours of the fabulous wealth of Croesus, which then found its way into the coffers of Cyrus, may have reached the prophet."

It is obvious that the above three commentators are approaching the subject of the "treasures of darkness and hidden riches of secret places" from different angles. What is clear and runs as a common thread through all three commentators though are two things. The first one is that, these treasures of darkness and hidden riches of secret places were not only from Babylon but from other nations as well. The second common thread that the commentators agree on is that these are subterranean treasures. They are deliberately hidden and concealed underground.

When King Cyrus conquered Babylon, he restored the vessels of the house of the LORD. The Bible says; *"Also Cyrus the king brought forth the vessels of the house of the LORD, which Nebuchadnezzar had brought forth out of Jerusalem, and had put them in the house of his gods; Even those did Cyrus king of Persia bring forth by the hand of Mithredath the treasurer, and numbered them unto Sheshbazzar, the prince of Judah." (Ezra 1v7-8)*

After restoring the treasures of the house of the LORD, King Cyrus must have remained with quite a hefty surplus of the treasures retrieved from the secret storages of Babylon. He must have remained with all the treasures and riches that were dispossessed from the kings of Edom, Moab, Ammon, Tyrus, Zidon and all the other nations that were conquered by the king of Babylon. Over and above this, King Cyrus remained with the treasures that were originally from Babylon.

Things will not be different with today's release of the Cyrus Anointing. The most important thing though is for those who are called and anointed with the Cyrus Anointing to espouse the fact that God promised to "**give**" these treasure of darkness and hidden riches of secret places to King Cyrus. "**Give**" is the operative word in this sense. In the same manner that God "**gave**" Jericho to the Israelites so He will "**give**" treasures of darkness and hidden riches of secret places to those anointed with the Cyrus Anointing today.

This means that, it is critical for those called and anointed with the Cyrus Anointing to hear God first concerning that which God has "**given**" to them. This will protect the saints called and anointed with the Cyrus Anointing from falling into the trap of greed and being lured by the deceptiveness of riches. This will create a balance in the lives of such believers that are called and anointed with the Cyrus Anointing.

The balance that is created comes from understanding that these treasures of darkness and hidden riches of secret places are not given just to anyone. They are given to those who are called *for Jacob my servant's sake and Israel mine elect, I have even called thee by thy name.* In other words, these treasures of darkness are given to those that will be actively engaged with the winning of souls and setting free of the people of God from satanic bondages.

It is also very important to realise that these treasures of darkness and hidden riches of secret places, will be "**given**" by God, they will not just fall on your lap. This is just like Jericho did not just fall on the lap of Joshua and the Israelites. They had to strictly adhere to the instructions of God Almighty in order for Jericho to fall. The same will be required of those to whom God "**gives**" treasures of darkness and hidden riches of secret places. In some instances, you may have to engage in intense spiritual warfare just like both the Israelites and Cyrus had to engage in a physical warfare to possess the land that God "**gave**" them.

As God, leads them to conquer they will also receive the same treasures of darkness and hidden riches of secret places. Some of these treasures will be treasures that are hidden in subterranean secret storages. As I related in an earlier chapter, early this year I had a dream. In the dream I had, I was in a farm that is owned by one of South Africa's wealthiest business person. In the dream, he was showing me this vault that was buried under the gravel drive way of his farm. This vault looked like a rectangular shaped container that was approximately one metre deep, five metres long and three metres wide. It had hydraulic arms that enabled it to be easily opened at the pressing of a button and it was filled to capacity with gold bars, silver bars, expensive and rare jewellery, diamonds, platinum and even a lot of US Dollars currency.

Because of the above dream, it is my belief that the treasures of darkness and hidden riches of secret places will come in different formats including buried treasures and riches as related in the above dream. I also believe that these treasures of darkness and hidden riches of secret places will come in the form of prophetic revelation of mineral resources and oil well.

A number of years back, a bus I was travelling on from King Williams Town to Port Elizabeth stopped next to an open field due to road construction. As I looked into the open field through the window, the Holy Spirit spoke to me and said; "there's oil on this field". In his book; "The Seven Mountain Prophecy", Johnny Enlow makes reference to how he prophesied that several mines; including gold, silver, salt, oil and many others would be discovered in Peru.

I also believe that the other manner in which these treasures will be discovered will be through God enabling believers to conquer and take over domains and institutions, only to discover that there are forgotten financial reserves that belong to these institutions. There will be investments that the previous owners thought would never be profitable. With the change in ownership, they will receive notifications of investment pay-outs that they did not even expect.

This will happen after they have taken the portion that God instructs them to take and dedicate unto Him. Once that dedication of that which is of God is done, it will release a whole lot more of the treasures of darkness and hidden riches of secret places. Some will purchase lands to build and during construction phase, discoveries of buried treasures will be made. There will be a lot of unusual wealth discoveries that will be made by the Cyrus Anointing.

These treasures of darkness and hidden riches of secret places will not only be limited to money. They will include that but will be much more than just money. The Cyrus Anointing will also discover rare minerals and oil wells. Those called and anointed with the Cyrus Anointed will be appointed by God Almighty to explore and also steward these resources for the glory of God Most High.

This will be a divine end time transfer of wealth. The Cyrus Anointing will find favour with some of the wealthiest men and women in the world. These wealthy and men and women will have their hearts turned towards those that are anointed with the Cyrus Anointing. As a result of that, they will voluntarily share their wealth with those that are walking in the Cyrus Anointing. Others will leave all their wealth to those that walk in the Cyrus Anointing by means of a will. Remember, the Bible says; *"The king's heart is in the hand of the LORD, as the rivers of water: he turneth it whithersoever he will."* **(Proverbs 21v1)**

CONFIRMATION OF GOD'S CALLING

God says that He gives the treasures of darkness and hidden riches of secret places to Cyrus so that Cyrus would know that it is God Himself that called him. This is so that Cyrus will in no way have any doubt whatsoever. It is my personal belief that this is so because of the measure of abundance of the wealth that God Almighty gave to King Cyrus.

This is how those that are called and anointed with the Cyrus Anointing will know for sure that God has called them. The mark and sign of the call of God upon their lives will be super abundant wealth. It will be the inexplicable, extreme, immeasurable and unfathomable wealth. It is wealth that is not achievable by human strength, skill, wisdom and knowledge. It will be obvious that the hand of God of Israel is on the Cyrus Anointing to prosper it.

Anyone and everyone that comes across the Cyrus Anointing will know instantaneously that the wealth possessed by those walking in and anointed with the Cyrus Anointing is wealth that can only be given by God Almighty. It will be so evident to an extent that even people that do not know God, will say it is impossible to attain such wealth with human strength and wisdom. Because of this naked evidence of the hand of God, many will be won over to Christ.

It is also worth noting that these treasures of darkness and hidden riches of secret places will be "**given**" to those that are called and anointed with the Cyrus Anointing. They will not have to toil or work hard for these treasures of darkness and hidden riches of secret places. It is also very critical to mention that those called and anointed with the Cyrus Anointing will be focused on executing the counsel of God and not focused on money.

It is this focus on executing the counsel of God that will qualify them to be "**given**" treasures of darkness and hidden riches of secret places by God. This is very critical as the One who will judge their hearts and readiness to be entrusted with the treasures of darkness and hidden riches of secret places is Almighty God Himself.

Chapter Ten

Cyrus – God's Battle Axe and Weapons of War

"Thou art my battle axe and weapons of war: for with thee will I break in pieces the nations, and with thee will I destroy kingdoms; And with thee will I break in pieces the horse and his rider; and with thee will I break in pieces the chariot and his rider; With thee also will I break in pieces man and woman; and with thee will I break in pieces old and young; and with thee will I break in pieces the young man and the maid; I will also break in pieces with thee the shepherd and his flock; and with thee will I break in pieces the husbandman and his yoke of oxen; and with thee will I break in pieces captains and rulers. And I will render unto Babylon and to all the inhabitants of Chaldea all their evil that they have done in Zion in your sight, saith the LORD."
(Jeremiah 51v20-24)

Most people make the mistake of thinking that the above quoted scriptural text is referring to Babylon. It is not only individuals that make this tragic mistake. It is also several Bible translations (with the exception of, in as far as I know, the Amplified and New Living Translation) that attribute the above quoted scripture to Babylon. This is a tragic mistake.

You may be asking "how did you reach that conclusion"? Let me explain how I reached that conclusion.

Firstly, let me state that both Jeremiah chapters 50 and 51 are about God's judgment on Babylon. Now, when reading verse 20 of Jeremiah chapter 51, you notice that the first part of the verse is in the present tense. God says; *"Thou art my battle axe and weapons of war:...".* He does not say that *"Thou hath been my battle axe and weapons of war..".*

If you look at Jeremiah 51v7 though, you will notice that, this verse that refers to Babylon is written in the past tense. It says; *"Babylon hath been a golden cup in the LORD's hand, that made all the earth drunken: for the nations have drunken of her wine; therefore the nations are mad."*

Just about every single verse that is made in reference to Babylon is written in the past tense. The other verse that shows us that God's battle axe and weapons of war is not Babylon is verse 24 of Jeremiah 51. It is my unwavering belief that this verse addresses Cyrus, God's battle axe and weapons of war. It says that Cyrus will witness all that which God will do to Babylon. He will have a "front row seat". Lastly, Babylon couldn't possibly be praised in the manner in which God's battle axe and weapons of war is being praised when it is also being judged.

God's Battle Axe

Just as the name suggests, a battle axe is used in a battle. It is an axe that is designed specifically for battle and is different from the normal axe that is used for the removal of trees.

Battle axes come in different shapes and sizes. Some are small and can be swung with one hand whilst others require both hands to swing.

It is God's plan to swing those He has called and anointed with the Cyrus Anointing as a battle axe against the enemy. The Cyrus Anointing will be in the forefront of the battle against the enemy. It (the Cyrus Anointing) will confront forces of darkness first hand. Those anointed with the Cyrus Anointing are guaranteed to have victory because it is God Almighty that swings them. The Cyrus Anointing is a weapon in the hand of God Almighty.

As a weapon in the hand of God, they do not get to choose how they want to be swung. They cannot dictate to the One that is using them in battle. This is because they are not the one with the knowledge of combat and the battle. Remember, God is a mighty warrior. He is great in battle. His name is the LORD.

Break In Pieces the Nations

God promises to break in pieces the nations with Cyrus. As we have seen in the Bible, God did indeed break in pieces the nations with King Cyrus. He used King Cyrus to conquer and defeat many nations of the earth including Babylon.

Today's release of the Cyrus Anointing will destroy and pulverise everything that the nations of the earth find pride in. This is all the stuff that keeps the nations of the earth from knowing and worshipping God in the right Way. The Cyrus

Anointing will be used to strip the nations of all their pride and the things that they find refuge in.

This is so that the nations will be able to realise their nakedness and poverty. Once they realise their nakedness and poverty, they will be turned towards God Almighty and begin to seek God. This will be when all their laws and financial systems and institutions of governance are failing. They will be failing because they are broken down by the Cyrus Anointing.

Destroy Kingdoms

There are many spiritual kingdoms that have established themselves over many regions, cities, nations and economic domains such as education, business, government, and other sectors of society. These are demonic kingdoms that have entrenched themselves in these domains and perverted these domains. They are under the control of the devil and therefore influence these domains in an ungodly manner.

The Cyrus Anointing is being released to confront and destroy these evil kingdoms. The Cyrus Anointing will wrestle, defeat and destroy these satanic kingdoms. It will redeem these domains and bring them under the rule and governance of Jesus Christ. Even the arts and entertainment industries will be redeemed. This will be done by means of spiritual warfare and the issuing of decrees that are irreversible.

Break In Pieces Horse and Rider

There are horses of the kingdom of darkness. These horses of the kingdom of darkness empower the workers of the work of the devil. These are riders of these spiritual demonic horses. They are agents of the devil in the different domains that we mentioned above. They are used by the devil to continually renew and strengthen the control of the devil over these territories and domains. They do this by performing secret satanic rituals. These rituals renew and strengthen the hold of the devil in these sectors. They keep the gate open to the devil so he can continue to influence these domains.

The Cyrus Anointing will discern these agents. Once they are discerned, the Cyrus Anointing will break their hold over the domains by prayer and spiritual warfare. They will be bound and stripped off their armour. All their works will be cancelled, reversed and nullified by the Cyrus Anointing. Those that are smart will repent, others will die because they refused to repent and accept Jesus Christ.

Break in Pieces the Chariot and his Rider

The workers of darkness also work in teams. They work in cells also. That is why God says He will, with King Cyrus, destroy the chariot and his rider.

The Cyrus Anointing will confront and destroy these teams of the devil that are working in different domains. These are cell groups that are working in companies, institutions, sectors, industries, cities, regions and nations. They are working together in advancing the demonic agenda. They bewitch the people of God with their charms and spells.

The Cyrus Anointing is endowed with the ability to discern their activities and also identify the members of such satanic cell groups. Once they have discerned and identified these satanic agents, they will destroy them and their works. They will engage in spiritual warfare and loose the grip of the devil on these domains mentioned above herein.

Break In Pieces Man and Woman

Both man and woman shall be broken in pieces by the Cyrus Anointing. They shall be shattered. All that which they have relied on shall be shattered and destroyed. All the wealth and possessions that they have built their lives on shall be stripped from them. They shall be left desolate. They shall be left destitute and naked.

This sorry state of affairs is what will remind them that they cannot save themselves. When their man-made fortresses are destroyed, they will realise that they are feeble mortal beings. In their state of brokenness, they will realise that they need a Saviour. It is in this state that their hearts will be turned and made pliable to the LORD God Almighty. This is how they will come to know Jesus Christ, the Lord of lords and King of kings.

This will be an individual experience for the man and the woman. All of the above will also apply to both the youth and the elderly. It will be the same experience for the young man as it will be for the young woman.

Break in Pieces the Shepherd and His flock

The Cyrus Anointing will dismantle the leaders and their followers. All the leaders that are leading people in wrong belief systems and wrong conduct will be broken to pieces. They will see their shame and nakedness. Once they see their shame and nakedness, they will be able to repent and find the LORD. This means that entire institutions and organizations will be reached and brought under the Lord Jesus Christ.

Break in Pieces the Husbandman and His Yoke of Oxen

The Cyrus Anointing will also break in pieces the husbandman and his yoke of oxen. All those that are leaders in government, businesses and other sectors will be broken to pieces by the Cyrus Anointing. It is not only them that will be broken to pieces but their workforce too will be broken to pieces.

They shall be subdued and brought under the rulership of Jesus Christ of Nazareth. In that way, the work that they were doing without God will now be aligned to the purpose, will and counsel of God. Their work will be redeemed and used for the advancement of the kingdom of God Almighty.

Break in Pieces Captains and Rulers

Captains and rulers in all spheres and sectors will be broken to pieces by the Cyrus Anointing. Those that are in positions of leadership and authority will also be subdued and brought under the rule and reign of Jesus Christ of Nazareth.

This will mean that they are now aligned to the will, counsel and purpose of God concerning the positions that they occupy. These will be leaders in government, business, academia, judiciary and all other sectors of society.

Chapter Eleven

Resident Authority in the Cyrus Anointing

"Now in the first year of Cyrus king of Persia, that the word of the LORD spoken by the mouth Jeremiah might be accomplished, the LORD stirred up the spirit of Cyrus king of Persia, that he made a proclamation throughout all his kingdom, and put it also in writing, saying, Thus saith Cyrus king of Persia, All the kingdoms of the earth hath the LORD God of heaven given me; and he hath charged me to build him an house in Jerusalem, which is in Judah. Who is there among you of all his people? The LORD his God be with him, and let him go up." **(2 Chronicles 36v22-23)**

"Now in the first year of Cyrus king of Persia, that the word of the LORD spoken by the mouth Jeremiah might be accomplished, the LORD stirred up the spirit of Cyrus king of Persia, that he made a proclamation throughout all his kingdom, and put it also in writing, saying, Thus saith Cyrus king of Persia, All the kingdoms of the earth hath the LORD God of heaven given me; and he hath charged me to build him an house in Jerusalem, which is in Judah. Who is there among you of all his people? His God be with him, and let him go up to Jerusalem, which is in Judah, and build the house of the LORD God of

> *Israel, (he is the God,) which is in Jerusalem. And whosoever remaineth in any place where he sojourneth, let the men of his place help him with silver, and with gold, and with goods, and with beasts, beside the freewill offering for the house of God that is in Jerusalem."* ***(Ezra 1v1-4)***

God stirred up the spirit of King Cyrus and made King Cyrus to issue a decree. The decree that King Cyrus made was for the rebuilding of the house of the LORD in Judah. He did not end there but he also released the Israelites that were held captive in Babylon. He released them so that they can be able to go and build the house of the LORD in Judah.

The interesting thing about the decree issued by King Cyrus is that his decree was irreversible. The decrees issued by the kings of the Medes and Persians were not to be altered by anyone, even by succeeding kings. We see evidence of this in the Bible on more than one occasion. The first occasion was when the enemies of Israel tried to oppose the rebuilding of the temple of God. The Bible says;

> *"Now when the adversaries of Judah and Benjamin heard that the children of the captivity builded the temple unto the LORD God of Israel; Then they came to Zerubbabel, and to the chief of the fathers, and said unto them, Let us build with you: for we seek your God, as ye do; and we do sacrifice unto him since the days of Esar-haddon king of Assur, which brought us up hither. But Zerubbabel, and Jeshua, and the rest of*

*the chief of the fathers of Israel, said unto them, Ye have nothing to do with us to build an house unto our God; but we ourselves together will build unto the LORD God of Israel, as King Cyrus the king of Persia hath commanded us. Then the people of the land weakened the hands of the people of Judah, and troubled them in building, And hired counsellors against them, to frustrate their purpose, all the days of Cyrus king of Persia, even until the reign of Darius king of Persia." **(Ezra 4v1-5)***

The Israelites continued to build the temple of the LORD God Almighty as they were commanded by King Cyrus. When the enemies of Israel noticed that the building of the temple was taking shape, they opposed the building of the temple.

The enemies of Israel went as far as writing letters to the king that was ruling in Persia at that time. The ruling king of that time was king Artaxerxes. They wrote to the king about how the rebuilding of the city of Jerusalem posed a threat to the kingdom and authority of the king. They even requested that the king orders that search be made in the royal archives so as to establish the threat that Jerusalem posed before it fell.

The king ordered and a search was done indeed. They found that the city of Jerusalem was a resilient city that conquered and was impossible to control until such time that God allowed their defeat after they (Israel) had sinned against God. This shocking discovery prompted the king to put a stop to the rebuilding project.

After a while, God stirred up the prophets Haggai and Zechariah. It was these two prophets that began to prophesy the word of the LORD to the people of Israel. Their prophesying encouraged the Israelites to recommence with the rebuilding project. They had left the building project until there was a new king in Persia. The new king was king Darius.

When their enemies came back and demanded to know who had given the Israelites permission to commence with the rebuilding of Jerusalem and the temple. They responded with wisdom this time around. They invoked the Cyrus Decree and told their adversaries the following;

> *"And they returned us answer, saying, We are the servants of the God of heaven and earth, and build the house that was builded these many years ago, which a great king of Israel builded and set up. But after our fathers had provoked the God of heaven unto wrath, he gave them into the hand of Nebuchadnezzar the king of Babylon, the Chaldean, who destroyed this house, and carried the people away into Babylon. But in the first year of Cyrus the king of Babylon the same King Cyrus made a decree to build this house of God. And the vessels also of gold and silver of the house of God, which Nebuchadnezzar took out of the temple that was in Jerusalem, and brought them into the temple of Babylon, those did Cyrus the king take out of the temple of Babylon, and they were delivered unto one, whose name was Sheshbazzar, whom he had made*

governor; And said unto him, Take these vessels, go, carry them into the temple that is in Jerusalem, and let the house of God be builded in his place. Then came the same Sheshbazzar, and laid the foundation of the house of God which is in Jerusalem: and since that time even until now hath it been in building, and yet it is not finished. Now therefore, if it seem good to the king, let there be search made in the king's treasure house, which is there at Babylon, whether it be so, that a decree was made of Cyrus the king to build this house of God at Jerusalem, and let the king send his pleasure to us concerning this matter." ***(Ezra 5v11-17)***

Thank God Almighty for the ministry of the prophets Haggai and Zechariah. It is their prophesying that encouraged the people of Israel to resume with the building project even though they did not have the permission from king Darius. They knew that they had the permission of the KING of Kings given to them through the mouth of King Cyrus.

It was the prophetic ministry of Haggai and Zechariah that gave them this boldness to resume the building project. It is also this prophetic ministry that enabled them to respond with wisdom when their enemies began to frustrate their building efforts. Because of the prophetic ministry of Haggai and Zechariah they were able to invoke the Cyrus Decree.

Upon the enemies of Israel writing a letter to inform king Darius that the Israelites have resumed the building project and, that they (Israelites) claimed that they are building as per the decree made by King Cyrus, King Darius ordered that a search be made in the royal archives so they could establish the veracity of the claims of the Israelites. Search was indeed made and they discovered that King Cyrus did indeed make that decree.

On hearing this, King Darius ordered that, Tatnai the governor, Shethar-boznai, and all others that opposed Israel in their building project, to keep their distance and no longer interrupt the building of the house of God. He did one better and also made a decree of his own. The Bible tells us that he said;

> *"Moreover I make a decree what ye shall do to the elders of these Jews for the building of this house of God: that of the king's goods, even of the tribute beyond the river, forthwith expenses be given unto these men, that they be not hindered. And that which they have need of, both young bullocks, and rams, and lambs, for the burnt offerings of the God of heaven, wheat, salt, wine, and oil, according to the appointment of the priests which are at Jerusalem, let it be given them day by day without fail: That they may offer sacrifices of sweet savours unto the God of heaven, and pray for the life of the king, and of his sons. Also I have made a decree, that whosoever shall alter this word, let timber be pulled down from his house, and being set up, let him be hanged thereon; and let his house be made a dunghill for this. And the God that hath caused his name to dwell there destroy all kings and people that shall put to their hand to alter and to destroy this house of God which is at*

Jerusalem. I Darius have made a decree; let it be done with speed." (Ezra 6v8-12)

King Darius did not only order those opposing the building project of Jerusalem and the house of God to stop opposing it. He went further and decreed that all the expenses for the building of the house of the LORD as well as all the priestly related expenses would come from the king's revenue collected by those that opposed the building project of the Israelites.

He even went further than that and also decreed that anyone that will alter the decree for the building of the house of the LORD would be hanged. They would not just be hanged but timber would be pulled from their house and be hanged with the very same timber. Further to that, Darius decreed that this person's house would be completely destroyed and turned into a dunghill.

This is the type of authority that is resident within the Cyrus Anointing. It is the power and authority to make decrees that are irreversible. Today's release of the Cyrus Anointing will see decrees being made over regions, cities, nations and sectors of the economy. These decrees will be responsible for the freeing of these regions, cities, nations and sectors.

The beauty of these decrees is that they are perpetual decrees. They are decrees that will never be changed. At times some generations may lose sight of and forget these decrees but they will be revived by the prophetic anointing. It will be the prophets that will encourage, enthuse and embolden the Church to arise and rebuild.

The Cyrus Decree will ensure the perpetual release of financial resources for the work of the Kingdom of God. Lack of money and finances for the work of God will be a thing of the past once those called and anointed with the Cyrus Anointing are stirred in their spirits to make decrees over nations, cities, regions, churches, businesses, families and all other sectors.

These decrees will eat into the financial resources of the ones that opposed those that are busy with the work of God. Just as King Darius decreed that all the expenses of the house of God be taken from revenue collected by Tatnai the governor that opposed the Israelites in their building project.

King Darius also decreed that God should destroy all kings and people that would want to alter and destroy the house of God which is in Jerusalem. This means that whosoever will fight against the decree made by the Cyrus Anointing would be fighting against God Almighty Himself. There is not a single person or spiritual entity that will fight against God and win. It is not even a contest.

King Darius also decreed that that which he decreed about the provisions of the house of God from the royal treasurery should be carried out speedily. This means that the decrees made by the Cyrus Anointing according to the law of the Medes and Persians which does not alter will be accelerated in their fulfilment. There will be no delays whatsoever in the carrying out of these decrees.

The angels of the LORD God Almighty will swiftly bring these decrees into fulfilment. Men and women will be divinely assigned to bring these decrees to pass. People that you do not know will come to you and say, I just want to give you this money; car, house, business or whatever else is needed for the fulfilment of the work of the house of God.

The Bible also says that;

> *"Then Tatnai, governor on this side of the river, Shethar-boznai, and their companions, according to that which Darius the king had sent, so they did speedily. And the elders of the Jews builded, and they prospered through the prophesying of Haggai the prophet and Zechariah the son of Iddo. And they builded, and finished it, according to the commandment of the God of Israel, and according to the commandment of Cyrus, and Darius, and Artaxerxes king of Persia."* ***(Ezra 6v13-14)***

The Cyrus Decree ensures that the work of God will be finished. The work of God will not be abandoned. This is the grace that is upon the Cyrus Anointing. It is to carry the work of God to its conclusion. The Cyrus Anointing will not cut corners or short change the assignment of God. This anointing is faithful to the call and assignment given to it by God Almighty. Just like apostle Paul that says; *"....I was not disobedient unto the heavenly vision:"* ***(Acts 26v19).***

Lastly, I want to emphasize that these decrees are not to be altered. These decrees are irreversible. The Bible says the following about these decrees;

*"If it please the king, let there go a royal commandment from him, and let it be written among the laws of the Persians and the Medes, that it be not altered, That Vashti come no more before king Ahasuerus; and let the king give her royal estate unto another that is better than she. And when the king's decree which he shall make shall be published throughout all his empire, (for it is great) all the wives shall give to their husbands honour, both to great and small." **(Esther 1v19-20)***

"Now, O king, establish the decree, and sign the writing, that it be not changed, according to the law of the Medes and Persians, which altereth not. Wherefore king Darius signed the writing and the decree. Now when Daniel knew that the writing was signed, he went into his house; and his window being open in his chamber toward Jerusalem, he kneeled upon his knees three times a day, and prayed, and gave thanks before his God, as he did aforetime. Then these men assembled, and found Daniel praying and making supplication before his God. Then they came near, and spake before the king concerning the king's decree; Hast thou not signed a decree, that every man that shall ask a petition of any God or man within thirty days, save of thee, O king, shall be cast into the den of lions? The king answered and said, The thing is true, according to the law of the Medes and Persians which altereth not. Then answered they and said before the king, That Daniel, which is of the children of the captivity of Judah, regardeth not thee,

O king, nor the decree that thou hast signed, but maketh his petition three times a day. Then the king, when he heard these words, was sore displeased with himself, and set his heart on Daniel to deliver him: and he laboured till the going down of the sun to deliver him. Then these men assembled unto the king, and said unto the king, <u>Know, O king, that the law of the Medes and Persians is, That no decree nor statute which the king establisheth may be changed.</u> Then the king commanded, and they brought Daniel, and cast him into the den of lions. Now the king spake and said unto Daniel, Thy God whom thou servest continually, he will deliver thee. And a stone was brought and laid upon the mouth of the den; and the king sealed it with his own signet, and with the signet of his lords; that the purpose might not be changed concerning Daniel." (Daniel 6v8-17)

In conclusion, I am certain that you can clearly see from these scriptures that the decrees made in accordance to the law of the Medes and Persians cannot be altered. They are irreversible. This kind of power and authority calls for those that are anointed with the Cyrus Anointing to be very mature leaders. They are not to be babies in Christ.

The reason for this demand for maturity and sound judgment stems from the fact that they have to handle enormous power and authority. This kind of power and authority requires that one is highly responsible for their actions and utterances. This is because if this authority and power is not discharged in a responsible manner, it can cause very serious damage.

As we have read, even though king Darius, wanted to save and deliver Daniel from being thrown into the den of lions, he could not do so. This is because these decrees are irreversible. King Darius could not even reverse a decree that he made himself.

Because of the severity of the authority to make decrees according to the law of the Medes and Persians which does not alter, those called and anointed with the Cyrus Anointing will need to develop a very deep relationship of intimacy with God. They will need to hear the voice of God very clearly. This will keep them from making irresponsible decrees that will cause havoc and damage that is not intended by God.

Chapter Twelve

The Army Marshalled By Cyrus

King Cyrus did not conquer Babylon by himself. He was a leader and a commander of the army of God. At this point in time, I want us to look into the characteristics and traits of the army that was marshalled and led by King Cyrus. There are several scriptures that give us a glimpse into the characteristics and traits of the army led by King Cyrus. The first one that we will look at reads as follows;

> *"I have commanded my sanctified ones, I have also called my mighty ones for mine anger, even them that rejoice in my highness. The noise of a multitude in the mountains, like as of a great people; a tumultuous noise of the kingdoms of nations gathered together: the LORD of hosts mustereth the host of the battle. They come from a far country, from the end of heaven, even the LORD, and the weapons of his indignation, to destroy the whole land."* ***(Isaiah 13v3-5)***

Sanctified Ones

Sanctification is the trade mark of those that form part of the army of God marshalled by the Cyrus Anointing. To sanctify means to make holy and set apart for one specific use and purpose. In this case, it refers to those whom God set apart for the purpose of inflicting His judgment on Babylon. It is God Almighty that reserved them for this particular task and purpose.

Today, those that are called and anointed to form part of the army led by the Cyrus Anointing are also set apart by God for the same task of destroying and dismantling every system of the world that is opposed to God. They are set apart to destroy every work of the devil and every single thing that is opposed to the will and counsel of God.

For the New Testament believers that are called to form part of the army that is under the command of the Cyrus Anointing, it will not be enough to be set apart by God. Those believers also have the responsibility of ensuring that they purify themselves. The reason for this is because, it is possible to step aside and be disobedient whilst set apart by God's predetermined will and counsel.

That is why it becomes imperative that each believer hoping to form part of the army led by the Cyrus Anointing and therefore manifest a degree of the Cyrus Anointing to continually purify themselves. The Bible says; *"And every man that hath this hope in him purifieth himself, even as he is pure." (1John 3v3).* Continuously purifying themselves will keep them from distractions and ensure that they do not become a defiled vessel.

The vessels that carry the mandate of God must be purified. It is this state of being continuously purified that will also shield them from the devil. It brings about the divine protection of God. Any form of sin and defilement breaks the hedge of protection in all believer's lives. Remember the Bible says; *"..and whoso breaketh an hedge, a serpent shall bite him." (Ecclesiastes 10v8).*

Mighty Ones

The army led by King Cyrus is a mighty army. They are strong. These are not weak and petty individuals. They have been thoroughly trained and equipped for battle. Their strength and resilience has been built through many years of intensive military training. They are competent in the use of the sword in the fight against the enemy.

For those called to be part of this army today, it is no different. The only difference is that today's army led by the Cyrus Anointing will be trained and equipped in the school of the Spirit. Their skills in spiritual warfare will be honed through intensely difficult circumstances, time spent in prayer and the study of the Word of God.

They will learn to handle the Sword of the Spirit. They will put on the whole armour of God found in Ephesians chapter 6. Not only that, they will have to edify and build themselves up in the spirit by praying in tongues always. This exercise of praying in tongues will strengthen them with might in the inner man. It will build up their boldness and courage in confronting the powers of darkness and defeating them all the time.

Them that Rejoice in My Highness

Satisfaction and joy is only derived by these individuals in the highness of God. They rejoice only when God Almighty and all His purposes are lifted up and exalted in the earth. That is why they will not rest one bit until such time that God is exalted in all the earth. They are not satisfied with the mere lip service in exalting God. They really want to bring every single domain under the rule of God in the literal sense.

It is this type of army that will help advance the Kingdom of God in the earth today. They will help to prepare the ground for the coming of Lord Jesus Christ. This they will do by ensuring the restitution of all things. Remember, the Bible says; *"And he shall send Jesus Christ, which before was preached unto you: <u>Whom the heaven must receive until the times of restitution of all things</u>, which God hath spoken by the mouth of all his holy prophets since the world began." (Acts 3v20-21).*

The Bible teaches us that; *"The earth is the LORD's, and the fullness thereof; the world, and they that dwell therein." (Psalm 24:1).* It is critical that we all remember that God entrusted the earth to Adam but Adam gave away his authority and stewardship over the earth to the devil.

Our Lord Jesus Christ redeemed us and restored us to the place of authority and stewardship over the earth. That is why now the responsibility to ensure that all things are restored and brought back under the Lordship of Jesus Christ falls on the Church of Jesus Christ. It is only once all things are restored and brought under the Lordship of Jesus Christ will

Jesus Christ return. It is only once the Church walks in the dominion mandate of Genesis 1:28 when it has subdued and has dominion over all creation. This is what them that rejoice in His Highness will make a reality in our life time.

A Multitude in the Mountains

It is not a few people that are in this army led by the Cyrus Anointing. This is a multitude of men and women that are called by God Almighty. They are also positioned in mountains. Mountains represent the different sectors of society such as politics/government, media, education, business, Judiciary, and all the other economic and societal sectors.

They are multitudes that God Almighty has placed strategically in places of influence and decision making. These people will influence the formation of policies since they are already on the inside of the sectors and institutions that need to be redeemed and reclaimed back to the Church. Others who are not in positions of authority and influence will be granted wisdom by God. It is that wisdom that will usher them before kings and find promotions. They will be like Daniel, Hananiah (Shadrach), Mishael (Meshach) and Azariah (Abed-nego) in Babylon.

These multitudes shall not be quiet on these mountains. They shall continually make decrees and declarations to dislodge the powers of darkness in these domains. They will also testify about Jesus Christ and reach their colleagues for Christ. Their voice shall be heard as it will be dominant on these mountains. That is what will make them influence policy formation in these sectors.

A Great People

The company and army marshalled by King Cyrus constitutes of great people. They are a people of great stature and standing in their nations. They are honoured and revered because of the grace and gifts of God Almighty within them. It is these gifts bestowed by God on them that have ushered them to stand before kings and establish them as authorities and leaders in their field of calling and assignment.

They are great in the arts, education, medical sciences, technology, legal fields, aviation, business, media, politics & government, church leadership, and all the other sectors of society. Their greatness has earned them the respect and honour of the nation. As a people called to constitute part of the army marshalled by the Cyrus Anointing, they can expect to be promoted and elevated by God to a place of greatness.

This greatness is not intended for them to be exalted above other people. It is not intended for them to exalt themselves above others and be proud. This garment of greatness will be handed to them so that they can be able to influence policies in the land. It is meant to strategically place them so that they can be effective agents of the kingdom of God. They will execute their duties and mandate as ambassadors of the Kingdom of God.

Kingdoms of Nations Gathered Together

> *"For, lo, I will raise and cause to come up against Babylon an assembly of great nations from the north country:..".* ***(Jeremiah 50v9)***

Just like the army led by king Cyrus was an alliance consisting many nations, so will be the modern day army marshalled by the Cyrus Anointing. It will consist of believers from different nations and nationalities. They will all be united by one purpose and one mission. That is the purpose and mission of bringing an end to the evil and unjust system of Babylon, the world.

The Bible refers to them as *"a tumultuous noise of the kingdoms of nations"*. This is a noise that will be heard across the nations of the earth. There will be no suppressing it and there will be no snuffing it out. That is because, this generation that rises is the salt of the earth and the light of the world. The darkness in the world will be expelled by this unique breed that carries a heavenly mandate.

They are a tumultuous noise of the kingdoms of nations gathered together. This noise is heard across the entire spectrum of the nations of the earth. They are heard on a global scale. The Bible says; *"There is no speech nor language, where their voice is not heard. Their line is gone out through all the earth and their words to the end of the world."* ***(Psalm 19v3-4).***

Mustered By the LORD

The Bible goes on to say that; *"....the LORD of hosts mustereth the host of the battle."* To 'muster' means to 'put together'. It means to 'assemble'. More specifically in the context of this scripture, it means to 'assemble in battle formation'. The army commanded by King Cyrus was assembled and gathered by God Almighty Himself. It is God Almighty that enlisted those that constituted this army.

Today, it will be no different with the army that is led by the Cyrus Anointing. All those that constitute this army today will be assembled and put together in battle formation by God Almighty Himself. Their connections will be divine connections. None of them will be out of place because God knows exactly where each piece of the puzzle fits in and will be placed in its place by God. Not a single person will assume this responsibility without being called by God. Remember, the Bible says; *"And no man taketh this honour unto himself, but he that is called of God, as was Aaron." **(Hebrews 5v4)**.*

Because it is God that is assembling and putting this army together in battle formation, it means that there will be no issues of pettiness and quarrels among them. They will be like the stones that were used when King Solomon built the temple of God. These stones were prepared in the quarry so that during the building phase there was no noise or sound of any tool heard cutting stones into shape. The Bible says; *"And the house, when it was in building, was built of stone made ready before it was brought thither: so that there was neither hammer nor axe nor any tool of iron heard in the house, while it was in building." **(1 Kings 6v7)***

This army is much like the army of Joel chapter two. They leave a trail of destruction of all the works of the devil behind them. When they fall upon a sword, they do not get wounded. Meaning they don't get offended. They do not break ranks. They each run within the lane allocated them by the LORD. You are welcome to read more about the army of Joel chapter two, please read from verse 1 until verse 11.

Origin of this Army

The Bible says; *"They come from a far country, from the end of heaven, even the LORD, and the weapons of his indignation, to destroy the whole land." **(Isaiah 13v5).*** It is very clear that this breed of believers come from God Almighty Himself. They are released by Heaven itself. When God released their spirit man to be conceived in the belly of their mothers, God's purpose and intent was already in place.

This is not an army that is appointed and elected by people. It is not an army that is assembled by the church boards. They are called, anointed and assembled by the LORD God Almighty Himself. They are born of the Spirit, water and the Blood that came out when they stabbed Jesus Christ on the Cross of Calvary. They may not necessarily have the approval of man but they have the approval of and calling from God.

Immune to Financial Temptation

The army led by King Cyrus was immune to any form of financial temptation. They could not be bought or bribed at all. This is evident in the Bible because the Bible says;

> *"Behold, I will stir up the Medes against them, which shall not regard silver; and as for gold, they shall not delight in it."* ***(Isaiah 13v17).***

Today's army led and commanded by the Cyrus Anointing will not be susceptible to bribes. They cannot be tempted with silver and gold. This is because they are so faithful to the mandate and assignment of God upon their lives. They are accountable to God Almighty Himself. They live their lives before God Almighty and not people. The fear of the LORD has become their treasure.

Nation from the North

The Bible says; *"For out of the north there cometh up a nation against her, which shall make her land desolate, and none shall dwell therein: they shall remove, they shall depart, both man and beast."* ***(Jeremiah 50v3).***

The army led and commanded by king Cyrus is referred to as the 'nation from the north'. This is because; they were from a country that was geographically located on the north of Babylon.

The north is a symbolic or metaphoric representation of Heaven. That is why the army led and commanded by the Cyrus Anointing today are from Heaven. They are from God Almighty Himself. This is exactly as explained above under the heading 'Origin of this Army', please refer to it.

Weapons of God's Indignation

The Bible says the following;

> *"..., and the weapons of his indignation, to destroy the whole land." **(Isaiah 13v5)***

> *"The LORD hath opened his armoury, and hath brought forth the weapons of his indignation: for this is the work of the Lord God of hosts in the land of the Chaldeans." **(Jeremiah 50v25).***

The release of the Cyrus Anointing is accompanied by the opening of the armoury of God. An armoury is the place wherein arms or weapons of war are kept. This army that God is raising has been kept locked up in God's weaponry depot and storage. They are called weapons of God's indignation.

A weapon of indignation is a weapon of wrath. It is released and only used to express the wrath and indignation of God. These weapons can be compared to modern day weapons of mass destruction. In the realm of the spirit, these weapons of God's indignation are like the weapons of mass destruction, only superior to weapons of mass destruction.

The Bible also states that these weapons of God's indignation are being brought out of God's armoury for the sole purpose of destroying the whole land of Babylon. They have a mandate to lay bare the whole system of the world that promotes greed and inequality. It is a system that enslaves the poor in debt. It is a system of ungodliness that is completely against God. It is a system that has shut God out of His own earth. The weapons of God's indignation are being raised in the earth to destroy this system.

Archers

The Bible says;

> "Call together the archers against Babylon: all ye that bend the bow, camp against it round about;.....".
> *(Jeremiah 50v29)*

There were archers in the army that was led by King Cyrus. Archery is an activity that requires excellent skill and precision. It deals with pinpointing a target and going after it. The most skilled of archers will hit the target on the "bull's eye" every time. The beauty of archery is that you can hit your target from a distance. Most of the time the target is not even aware that it is being stalked.

The army led and commanded by the Cyrus Anointing today is no different. It will consist of skilled archers that will stalk and target the Babylonian system with their apostolic decrees and prophetic declarations. These will be words of judgment and condemnation spoken against the system of the world. These words are so powerful because they will be spoken in agreement with God Almighty over the entire domain of darkness defiling the marketplace. Just as the archers target from a distance, so will these pronouncements of judgment be made from a distance.

I also believe that these archers will also be those that will invest in companies through the stock exchanges. They will not be involved in the day to day running of these entities but their ultimate goal will be to take over these companies. In order to achieve that, they will amass many shares undetected from a distance. At the appointed time, when they have acquired the controlling share, they will take over the running of these corporations.

A Destroying Wind

> *"Thus saith the LORD, Behold, I will raise up against Babylon, and against them that dwell in the midst of them that rise up against me, a destroying wind; And will send unto Babylon fanners, that shall fan her, and shall empty her land: for in the day of trouble they shall be against her round about."* **(Jeremiah 51v1-2)**

God refers to this army as 'a destroying wind'. This is wind that is meant to cause damage. It is meant to cause havoc and destruction. It is very important to remember that king Cyrus is called the righteous man from the east. If King Cyrus is from the east, then it is right to conclude that the army he led and commanded also came from the east.

This therefore means that this army led and commanded by the Cyrus Anointing will come against Babylon like the east wind of God. The east wind of God is a tool, weapon and technology that God uses when He wants to bring destruction and misery to a place. Remember when God sent His east wind against Egypt? The Bible says; *"And Moses stretched forth his rod over the land of Egypt, and the LORD brought an east wind upon the land all that day, and all that night; and when it was morning, the east wind brought the locusts."* **(Exodus 10v13)**. Just like the east wind of God that brought locusts upon Egypt, so will this army bring complete destruction on the system of the world.

In conclusion, this company of believers walking in the Cyrus Anointing will be used by God to mete out His judgment upon the ungodly system of the world. Others will be used to expose diabolical schemes that are made to appear legal but all the while are deliberately intended to keep certain people groups in perpetual bondage.

This army will come from all sectors and spheres of society. Others will come from finance, government, academics, engineering and many other sectors of the economy. Others will be graced with innovative abilities and they will bring out inventions that will undermine the schemes of the worldly system and uplift many people's lives.

Chapter Thirteen

Cyrus - the Prophetic Shadow of Jesus Christ

In the process of receiving and propagating new revelations and truths to the Church, it is very critical and prudent for every believer and/or preacher to ensure that that new revelation eventually points us to Jesus Christ. It is important to ensure that our message does not depart from Christ and that at all times it remains Christ Centred. Anything otherwise it is no longer the gospel.

This understanding stems from knowing that the whole Bible, from Genesis to Revelations, is about Jesus Christ the Son of the Living God. It also stems from knowing and understanding that the Bible is a prophetic book. Because, the Bible is a prophetic book, the language thereof is also a prophetic language. The language of the Bible is; metaphors, dark speeches, allegories and similitudes.

It is with this background and understanding that I want us to look at and unlock Jesus Christ in the life of King Cyrus and also look at how that applies to modern day believers called and anointed with the Cyrus Anointing today. This we will do by looking at the parallels between the life of King Cyrus and that of King of kings Jesus Christ of Nazareth.

At the moment, we will only look at four parallels between King Cyrus and King of kings Jesus Christ the Son of the Living God. The parallels we will look at are; "Cyrus the

Anointed and Jesus Christ the High Priest", "Cyrus the Deliverer and Jesus Christ the Messiah", "Cyrus the Shepherd of the LORD and Jesus Christ the Chief Shepherd", and "The Cyrus Decree and The Word of God". Let us look at the first parallel;

Cyrus the Anointed - Jesus Christ the High Priest

> *"Thus saith the LORD to his anointed, to Cyrus, whose right hand I have holden, to subdue nations before him; and I will loose the loins of kings, to open before him the leaved gates; and the gates shall not be shut;...."* **(Isaiah 45:1)**

The story of the calling and commissioning of King Cyrus is an Old Testament account. It is a well-known fact that under the Old Testament, the anointing was reserved solely for those that were Israelites. Even within the nation of Israel, it was only the kings, prophets, priests and judges that could be anointed. Anyone else was disqualified from being anointed by God.

In the midst of all of this strict set up and divine regulation, God calls and anoints King Cyrus who was not just not an Israeli king, priest, prophet or judge but was a gentile. Gentiles were strictly prohibited and excluded from taking part in the sacred things of God. In fact, Paul the apostle states that;

> *"Don't forget that you gentiles used to be outsiders. You were called "uncircumcised heathens" by the*

*Jews, who were proud of their circumcision, even though it affected only their bodies and not their hearts. In those days you were living apart from Christ. You were excluded from citizenship among the people of Israel, and you did not know the covenant promises God had made to them. You lived in this world without God and without hope". **(Ephesians 2:11-12 NLT)***

The calling and commissioning of King Cyrus was as a result of the election and choosing of God. So critical and important was the purpose of God that it transcended and broke through the regulation so that God could anoint King Cyrus. This shows that God is not confined to the mind-set and limitations of mankind. As high as the heavens are from the earth, so are his thoughts and ways from our thoughts and ways.

Now, the parallel of this anointing and commissioning of King Cyrus, the gentile, is that of Jesus Christ being established as a high priest. According to the law of God given through Moses, priests were to come strictly from the house of Aaron the descendant of Levi. Apart from being from the house of Aaron and from the tribe of Levi, you were disqualified from becoming a priest. Because of the election and choosing of God, the establishment of a new and higher priesthood necessitated that once again the purpose of God transcends and breaks through the regulation.

By conquering Babylon and setting free the Israelites once, King Cyrus was pointing to the fact that Jesus Christ would offer Himself once off as a sacrifice for the sins of the world and establish the new priesthood. Unlike the Levitical priests that entered the most holy place once every year with the blood of bulls and bullocks, Jesus Christ entered (as a high priest) only once with His own Blood and redeemed all of mankind and reconciled us back to God. This was the establishment of the Melchizedek priesthood.

In the same manner that, though a gentile, King Cyrus was called and anointed by God; those who are called to walk in the Cyrus Anointing will come from unconventional backgrounds. Most of them will be a people that are despised and looked down upon. They do not necessarily have any man's endorsement or approval. They do not come from affluent families and/or backgrounds but the grace, favour and anointing of God upon their lives enables them to transcend the regulations and barriers of man. The purpose and election of God will upset and disrupt the status quo and promote them to places that others will say they don't deserve. They will be right in saying that but the favour of God will have made it possible.

Cyrus the Deliverer – Jesus Christ the Messiah

> *"For Jacob my servant's sake, and Israel mine elect, I have even called thee by thy name:..."* ***(Isaiah 45:4).***
>
> *".....and he shall let go my captives, not for price nor reward, saith the LORD of hosts."* ***(Isaiah 45:13).***

It was because of the completely dire state that Israel was in that it became necessary for God to raise, anoint and assign

King Cyrus to deliver Israel from slavery, bondage and servitude in Babylon. Israel was in a state of complete defeat. It was so bad so much that there was no one left in all of Israel and Judah that could lead the nation of Israel out of slavery in Babylon. It is critical to remember that Nebuchadnezzar the king of Babylon completely decimated Israel and Judah. The Bible says;

> *"At that time the servants of Nebuchadnezzar king of Babylon came up against Jerusalem, and the city was besieged. And Nebuchadnezzar king of Babylon came against the city, and his servants did besiege it. And Jehoiachin the king of Judah went out to the king of Babylon, he, and his mother, and his servants, and his princes, and his officers: and the king of Babylon took him in the eighth year of his reign. And he carried out thence all the treasures of the house of the LORD, and the treasures of the king's house, and cut in pieces all the vessels of gold which Solomon king of Israel had made in the temple of the LORD, as the LORD had said. And he carried away all Jerusalem, and all the princes, and all the mighty men of valour, even ten thousand captives, and all the craftsmen and smiths: <u>none remained, save the poorest sort of the people of the land</u>. And he carried away Jehoiachin to Babylon, and the king's mother, and the king's wives, and his officers, and the mighty of the land, those carried he into captivity from Jerusalem to Babylon. And all the men of might, even seven thousand, and craftsmen and smiths a thousand, all that were strong*

*and apt for war, even them the king of Babylon brought captive to Babylon". **(2Kings 24:10-16)***

*"But the captain of the guard left of the poor of the land to be vinedressers and husbandmen". **(2Kings 25:12)***

The above scriptures give us a very vivid picture of the extent of the damage inflicted by the king of Babylon upon the Israelites. It clearly outlines the various categories and groupings of people that were subdued and forcibly removed from their homeland into slavery. The actual "cream of the crop" is the ones that were defeated, subdued and hauled off to slavery.

We learn that the king, his servants, officers, craftsmen, mighty men of valour, those that were strong and apt for war and many others were taken to serve seventy years in slavery. These are the very people that were supposed to be the defenders of the nation but they got defeated, subdued and hauled off to slavery. Nebuzaradan, the captain of the guard for the king of Babylon left only the poorest sort of the people in Israel to tend the gardens.

The people that were left in Israel were already defeated long before Israel was subdued. They were not leaders or fighters. All that they were good for was to tend the garden. Their primary objective was survival as they were poor and had no thoughts of making a significant impact in life. They could not think beyond their immediate need for food and clothing.

Such a people could not deliver their brethren from Babylonian slavery. Hence the need for God to raise someone outside of Israel to rescue and deliver Israel out of their bondage. Israel had no heroes or mighty men that could come to their rescue. God raised up King Cyrus for this honourable task.

It is also worth noting that God says; *".....and he shall let go my captives, not for price nor reward, saith the LORD of hosts"*. The New Living Translation of the Bible reads as follow; *"....He will restore my city and free my captive people – without seeking a reward!"* This shows us that King Cyrus did not restore the city of God and free the Israelites for financial gain. He was never motivated by the prospect of self-enrichment.

Now, the prophetic parallel of this to Jesus Christ is the fact that Jesus Christ came as the Messiah. He came to seek and to save that which was lost. We all know that through the sin and disobedience of Adam; sin and disobedience came upon all mankind. This resulted in a situation wherein man died in his spirit.

Now, the spirit of man is the part that communes with God. When it died in Adam, Adam had children after his fallen nature. This was a state of broken fellowship with God wherein man now needed an intermediary to talk to God. The fellowship that Adam had with God in the Garden of Eden was broken. The Bible describes that state as; *"For all have sinned, and come short of the glory of God"* **(Romans 3:23).**

It is in this state of affairs that Jesus Christ came into the earth. The Bible teaches us that; *"For as in Adam all die, even so in Christ shall all be made alive"* **(1 Corinthians 15:22).** Christ found all of mankind dead in their sins through Adam's original sin. In this state, much like the Israelites in Babylon, mankind could not save themselves. Hence the Bible teaches us that; *"For God so loved the world, that he gave his only begotten Son, that whosoever believeth in him should not perish, but have everlasting life"* **(John 3:16).**

Just like King Cyrus never sought a reward for the work of rescuing and freeing the Israelites from Babylonian slavery, Thee King of kings, Jesus Christ of Nazareth the Son of the Living God never sought a reward for saving mankind. In fact, Jesus Christ had no benefit none whatsoever for rescuing us from our sins and the oppression of the devil.

Instead of Him requiring a reward, we see Jesus Christ saying; *"No one can take my life from me. I sacrifice it voluntarily. For I have the authority to lay it down when I want to and also to take it up again"* **(John 10:18).** This is definitely not the conduct of someone that is looking at getting a reward. Paul the apostle takes it further and tells us that; *"But God commendeth his love toward us, in that, while we were yet sinners, Christ died for us"* **(Romans 5:8).**

In the same manner, those who are called and anointed with the Cyrus Anointing will be deliverers. They will be a people that are concerned with winning souls. Reconciling entire nations to God will be their burning desire. It will be that which consumes them. This will stem from their understanding and internalization of Psalm 24:1.

They will be driven by their understanding that; *"The earth is the LORD's, and the fullness thereof; the world, and they that dwell therein"* **(Psalm 24:1).** This disposition of their hearts will compel them to want to win every single soul, domain, mountain or sector of society back to Christ. They will seek to redeem every sector back to God.

All of this, they will do without the need to be rewarded. Their treasure is found in doing the will of God and finishing it. They will *lay up for themselves treasures in heaven where moth and rust doth not corrupt and where thieves do not breakthrough and steal.* They will accomplish this by spending their resources and finances in funding the gospel. In obedience to Christ, they will give freely for they themselves have received freely.

Cyrus the Shepherd of the LORD – Jesus Christ the Chief Shepherd

> *"That saith of Cyrus, He is my shepherd, and shall perform all my pleasure: even saying to Jerusalem, Thou shalt be built; and to the temple, Thy foundation shall be laid"* **(Isaiah 44:28).**

By the election and calling of God, King Cyrus is called the "Shepherd of the LORD". He was the type of shepherd that received his shepherding mandate from the LORD God Almighty. His commissioning came from God and not from man. This means that there was a much higher and more stringent level of accountability and responsibility for King Cyrus. He needed to always be mindful of the fact that he had a heavenly calling. That necessitated that he lived his life before God Almighty.

Because of this higher and more stringent level of accountability and responsibility King Cyrus carried out his shepherding role with great care, fairness and justice. As a leader of an empire, King Cyrus is known to be a pioneer of human rights. According to historical record, the Cyrus Cylinder contained a framework from which the modern day human rights charter is modelled.

Fairness and justice were such popular hallmarks of his governance. History records that his opponents did not necessarily fight to the bitter end. The reason for that is because they knew King Cyrus to be a gracious victor. He allowed those he conquered to continue in self-governance. Though he introduced certain changes, certain things remained unchanged. He allowed things like freedom of religion.

The prophetic shadow of this to Jesus Christ is the fact that Jesus Christ is called the Chief Shepherd. If ever there was anyone that modelled submission to God the Father, it is Jesus Christ. The level of accountability to the Father and responsibility for His flock caused Jesus Christ to tell us that; *"I can of mine own self do nothing: as I hear, I judge: and my judgment is just; because I seek not mine own will, but the will of the Father which hath sent me"* **(John 5:30).**

Everything that Jesus Christ did, He did it in obedience to the Father. This is the leading attribute of a shepherd that is fully submitted and accountable to God. This is the highest level of humility. It demonstrates complete dependence and reliance on God. Jesus Christ modelled this greater than anyone ever. That is the level of Jesus Christ's submission to the will of the Father. The Bible tells us that Jesus Christ was so obedient to the Father to an extent that He humbled Himself to the point of death and death on the cross.

Whilst on earth, Jesus Christ remained so faithful to His shepherding responsibility to an extent that when He prayed in John 17 He said; *"……….: those that thou gavest me I have kept, and none of them is lost, but the son of perdition; that the scripture might be fulfilled"* ***(John 17:12).*** Ensuring the safety and well-being of those assigned to Him as a shepherd was Jesus Christ's delight. He gave an account to the Father to the effect that He had kept those the Father had entrusted to Him. This is the heartbeat of a genuine Shepherd.

Just like King Cyrus governed with fairness and justice, Jesus Christ also judges as He hears from the Father. Because of that, the judgment of Jesus Christ is just. In fact, the prophecy made by Isaiah about Jesus Christ tells us that; *"……….: and he shall not judge after the sight of his eyes, neither reprove after the hearing of his ears: But with righteousness shall he judge the poor, and reprove with equity for the meek of the earth:……."* ***(Isaiah 11:3-4).***

This is the very same example that those who are today called and anointed with the Cyrus Anointing are to follow. They need to live lives of accountability to God and responsibility for the flock that God Almighty entrusts to them. They are to be accountable and responsible for the assignment that God Almighty has given to them. In terms of their actions and pursuits, they are to be absolutely certain that they are only going after that which God has instructed them to go after. This will help ensure that they do not get side tracked.

Also, the manner in which they judge should not be fleshly. They should not be shepherds that weight people on the basis of their appearances but we are to judge as they hear from God. This means that they are going to need very high levels of discernment so that they can easily judge between the devils that come to them dressed very smartly and the angels that come to them dressed very shabby. This level of discernment will enable them to both protect the purpose of God from those with an evil agenda as well as to identify those that are sent by God and have genuine hearts for that which God is doing.

The Cyrus Decree – The Word of God

> *"And now, Your Majesty, issue and sign this law so it cannot be changed, an official law of the Medes and Persians that cannot be revoked"* ***(Daniel 6:8 NLT).***
>
> *"So if it please the king, we suggest that you issue a decree, a law of the Persians an Medes that cannot be revoked"* ***(Esther 1:19 NLT).***

One of the most interesting things about, not just King Cyrus but the Medo-Persian empire that he (King Cyrus) governed is the decrees made by the kings. As we have seen in the above two scriptures as well as the chapter on "The Resident Authority in the Cyrus Anointing"; the decrees made according to the law of the Medes and Persians are irreversible and cannot be altered.

The law of the Medes and Persians was so serious and strict to an extent that not even succeeding kings could alter the decrees made by their predecessors. As if that was not enough, according to the law of the Medes and Persians, a king could not even reverse or alter a decree that he had made himself. He was bound by the law of the Medes and Persians.

We saw that Medo-Persian kings could not even reverse, change, alter or revoke their own decrees in the case of Daniel. When King Darius was governing over Babylon, the; presidents and princes of Babylon conspired against Daniel because they could not compete with him in the work they had to do. The level of excellence that Daniel operated in was ten times better than them all (Daniel 1:20).

As a result of their (presidents and princes) inability to compete with Daniel, they conspired against him. Their conspiracy was so serious to an extent that they went as far as agreeing to trick King Darius into issuing a decree according to the law of the Medes and Persians. Such a decree was intended to prohibit everyone from praying to anyone but the king for a period of 30 days.

King Darius issued the decree as per the request of the presidents and princes. Naturally and true to his commitment to God, Daniel continued to pray to his God. The presidents and princes spied on him. Once they caught Daniel praying to

God, they reported him to the king. The king tried and did everything to try and save Daniel but the conspirators invoked the law of the Medes and Persians. That left the king with no choice but to have Daniel cast into the lion's den.

This is the extent of the strictness of the law of the Medes and Persians. There was no way to get around the decrees made according to the law of the Medes and Persians. Even the very king that made such a decree according to the law of the Medes and Persians was subject to and bound by the decree he made. This is just as we have seen in Daniel chapter six.

The impact of the decrees made according to the law of the Medes and Persians is that whatsoever was decreed by the king was established in perpetuity. Whatever was introduced through the decree made according to the law of the Medes and Persians was established forever in the Medo-Persian Empire. This was the creative power of these decrees.

Now this is parallel to Jesus Christ in that Jesus Christ is the Word of God. I want to quote a few scriptures that will give us a broader understanding of how the Cyrus Decree is a shadow of the reality that is found in Jesus Christ. The Bible says;

> *"Your word, LORD, is eternal; it stands firm in the heavens"* ***(Psalm 119:89 NIV)****.*

> *"Heaven and earth will pass away, but my words will never pass away"* ***(Luke 21:33 NIV)****.*

> *"………: for thou hast magnified thy word above all thy name"* ***(Psalm 138:2)****.*

It is clear from the above scriptures that; the perpetual stand and enforceability of the decrees made according to the law of the Medes and Persians, was symbolic of the Word of God. The Word of God is eternal. In other words, it transcends time, space and matter. It is not limited by the natural or physical realm. As such, it stands firm, unmoved and unshaken in the heavens.

Jesus Christ also tells us that; "heaven and earth shall pass away, but my words will never pass away". Just like the decrees of the Medes and Persians outlived and outlasted multiple generations, the Word of God outlasts and outlives everything. In fact, the Word of God is the very source of all life.

One of the things that we learn about the Word of God is that God has magnified His Word above His Name. It is not an insignificant thing for God to magnify His Word above His Name. This means that God is subject to His Word. He does not disobey His own Word. This is the same thing that we saw in Daniel chapter six. King Darius was subject to the decree that he made. He could not change his own decree.

Lastly, the Bible also teaches us that Jesus Christ is the Word of God. As the Word of God, Jesus Christ has been with God from eternity. All things were made by Him and without Him nothing that has been made was made.

Those who are called and anointed with the Cyrus Anointed are expected and required to bear a much higher standard. They are held to a much higher standard than any other person. Their level of honesty and integrity is to be above average. They are required to say what they mean and mean what they say. In the words of Jesus Christ, they are to; *"...let your yea be yea and your nay be nay.*

Lastly, as we have seen in the above outlined parallels, King Cyrus served as a prophetic shadow to King of kings, Jesus Christ the Son of the Living God. It is also evident in the Scriptures that though King Cyrus of old fulfilled his assignment of destroying Babylon, there remains a Babylon to be destroyed as seen in the book of Revelations.

This is why there is today a release and an outpouring of the very same grace and anointing that was upon King Cyrus. Those called to walk in and manifest the Cyrus Anointing need to fix their gaze on Jesus Christ for He is the real Deliverer and Messiah foreshadowed by King Cyrus.

Chapter Fourteen

Gearing for a Hostile Takeover

Make Bright the Arrows

> *"Make bright the arrows; gather the shields:...".* ***(Jeremiah 51v11)***

Making bright the arrows is the first step in gearing for a hostile takeover. Now, there is a threefold symbolic meaning of 'arrows'. At this point, I want to take some time and look at this threefold symbolic meaning of 'arrows' and see how this relates to us as the Church of Jesus Christ in the present day. Firstly, the Bible says;

> *"Lo, children are an heritage of the LORD: and the fruit of the womb is his reward. As arrows are in the hand of a mighty man; so are children of the youth. Happy is the man that hath his quiver full of them: they shall not be ashamed, but they shall speak with the enemies in the gate."* ***(Psalm 127v3-5).***

Arrows are Children

As you can see from the above quoted scripture, arrows are symbolic of children. The children that it is referring to are the children of God. This is both the young and the old that have been bought by the Blood of Jesus Christ the Lamb of God. The Bible says to *make bright the arrows.* It is my understanding that an arrow is at its brightest when it is sharpened.

The sharpening of the arrows that needs to be done is the teaching and spiritual equipping of the children of God that needs to be done. Once they are trained and equipped, they will be ready for the battle of attacking and destroying the spirit of Babylon wherever it manifests itself in the marketplace.

The Bible says that *children are an heritage of the LORD: and the fruit of the womb is his reward. As arrows are in the hand of a mighty man; so are children of the youth.* Those called and anointed with Cyrus Anointing will be entrusted with *children* to train and equip in the things of God. Once, they are thoroughly trained and equipped, they will be arrows in the hand of God.

This is because it is God Himself that will deploy them to specific sectors of the marketplace. This will be to any of the sectors of government, business, media, academia and all the other sectors. Because God is the 'mighty man' deploying and assigning them to their sectors, they will prosper in everything they do.

The quiver of God will be filled with these trained, skilled and equipped arrows. This will bring happiness to the LORD God Almighty. These arrows of God shall not be ashamed. They shall not be timid. They will not in any way show fear or draw back when dealing with the enemy.

The Bible says that *they shall speak with the enemies in the gate.* Now, gates represent the entryways. These are entryways in the realm of the spirit. These are gates that the devil has been controlling for many years. These gates bar many of the children of God from entering into different sectors of the marketplace.

These can be gates of prejudice, segregation, exclusion and other evils. They are meant to give access to a few people with a twisted, evil and selfish agenda. Remember that Jesus Christ says; *....upon this rock I will build my church; and the gates of hell shall not prevail against it.* These arrows will stand and advance against the gates of hell and the gates of hell will not stand against them. These arrows will both be offensive and defensive. They will be defensive in that they will watch the gates of their own city the Church of Jesus Chris.

Arrows are Apostolic Decrees and Prophetic Declarations

> *"The LORD also thundered in the heaven, and the Highest gave his voice; hailstones and coals of fire. Yea, he sent out his arrows, and scattered them; and he shot out lightnings, and discomfited them."* **(Psalm 18v13-14)**

> *"Shout against her round about:..".* **(Jeremiah 50v15)**

Arrows are projectiles. They function like missiles or like bullets. One of the key things to do as we are gearing for a hostile takeover of all the enemy occupied domains in the marketplace, we are to send forth the arrows. We are to not keep silent but to rather shout against Babylon.

We are to shout the apostolic decrees and prophetic declarations that dismantle all the kingdom of darkness and establish the rule of God Almighty in the earth today. This is a very critical component of the fight and battle for the control of the marketplace. It is critical for the Church to remember that; *"...the light shines in the darkness, and the darkness can never extinguish it."* **(John 1v5 NLT)**.

The apostolic and prophetic pronouncements that we make against Babylon are a light. It is this light that dispels and casts out all darkness. Remember, God spoke to the darkness and said, *"Let there be light"*. In the same manner, it will do us a lot of good to remember that the Bible says; *"Death and life are in the power of the tongue: and they that love it shall eat the fruit thereof."* **(Proverbs 18v21)**.

It is our responsibility to speak life into the marketplace. As we do that, darkness will be dispelled and cast out of the marketplace. This will establish the rule and reign of God Almighty and raise Jesus Christ as Lord of all.

Arrows Relate To Skill

Making bright the arrows also relates to polishing and sharpening the skill and talent that God Almighty has placed within you. This relates to both the anointing within you, natural talent and academically acquired skills. The skills need to be continuously polished and upgraded at all times. This will keep you on the 'cutting edge' and abreast of your counterparts in the marketplace. This will be excellence at its best.

Remember, Paul said to Timothy; *"Wherefore I put thee in remembrance that thou stir up the gift of God, which is in thee by the putting on of my hands."* ***(2 Timothy 1v6).*** It is the responsibility of each child of God to continuously polish and sharpen their skills. Their skills will be most effective when they are sharpened.

Gather the Shields

The Bible also says;

> *"...gather the shields..."*

It is my view that the shields that we are meant to gather are the protective promises of God. They are the promises of God that cover each and every aspect of your life from your physical health, mental & soul health, family well-being, financial well-being and all the other aspects of your life.

This is because, as we begin to mount an assault against the enemy, he will use every single dirty trick to try and distract us from executing the will and counsel of God. This therefore makes it very fundamental that each believer begins to know and understand the protective promises of God that will shield him/her from the attacks of the devil.

When a believer knows and understands these protective promises of God, he/she will be able to claim them every time the devil tries to distract you from your heavenly assignment. Believers will need to adopt and internalize John 10:10.

This will simplify the process of determining whether something comes from God or not. Without the knowledge of these protective promises of God, a believer will be going into battle 'naked' and will be the proverbial sitting duck for the devil and his demons.

Strategic Positioning

> *"Put yourselves in array against Babylon round about:..". (Jeremiah 50v14)*

When King Cyrus was ready to attack Babylon, he positioned his army all around Babylon. They surrounded the city of Babylon. In fact, when king Belshazzar of Babylon commanded that the vessels from the temple of God be brought for him to drink with his leadership (Daniel 5), the army of King Cyrus was already positioned around the city walls of Babylon.

They positioned themselves this way to ensure that no one escaped their sword. They positioned themselves that way to ensure that Babylon was completely destroyed. This is the same approach that the Church, the army of God is to position itself against modern day Babylon, the system of the world.

We are to camp within every sector of Babylon. This seed of believers will be positioned by God in every sector of society. They will be positioned in the entire marketplace. Others will be adjusted by God Himself. They are to be sensitive to the adjustment that God will be doing in their lives. God will adjust business people and cause them to preach. God will adjust preachers and cause them to do business.

This will require high levels of discernment and sensitivity to the Holy Spirit. Without this discernment and sensitivity to the Holy Spirit, others run the risk of missing or even rejecting that which God is doing. These adjustments are meant to strategically position the army of God in every single domain so as to subdue the evil princes and bring those particular domains under the Lordship of Jesus Christ.

Set Up the Standard

> *"Set up the standard upon the walls of Babylon, make the watch strong, set up the watchmen, prepare ambushes: for the LORD hath both devised and done that which he spake against the inhabitants of Babylon."* ***(Jeremiah 51v12)***

Setting Up the Standard

The setting up of the standard upon the walls of Babylon refers to the hoisting of the banner or flag of the army led and commanded by King Cyrus. King Cyrus and his army knew that Babylon was already given to them by God. That is why one of the first things they did was to hoist their own flag upon the walls of Babylon.

The interesting factor about this is that they hoisted their banner upon the walls of Babylon. This means that those watchmen from Babylon that stood on the walls to check for the enemy had already abandoned their positions. There was no one protecting Babylon from the coming army led by King Cyrus.

With today's release of the Cyrus Anointing, it will be no different. The Church will lift up Jehovah Nissi over the walls of Babylon. They will declare their victory over Babylon ahead of engaging in the physical capture of these domains. The reason why they will experience victory is because the Babylonian watchmen have already abandoned their positions. The Bible says; *"...she hath given her hand:..."*. *(Jeremiah 50v15)*. This means that Babylon surrenders.

Besides the hoisting of the banner, setting up the standard also refers to superseding the standards of Babylon. The standards of Babylon will be superseded by the establishment of Godly standards. Remember, God says; *"For my thoughts are not your thoughts, neither are your ways my ways, saith the LORD. For as the heavens are higher than the earth, so are my ways higher than your ways, and my thoughts than your thoughts." (Isaiah 55v8-9)*

It is not even a matter of discussion or negotiation that the standard of God far exceeds the standard of the world/Babylon. The setting up of the standard of God will be done by the Church of Jesus Christ. Remember that the Bible says;

> *"And it shall come to pass in the last days, that the mountain of the LORD's house shall be established in the top of the mountains, and shall be exalted above the hills; and all nations shall flow unto it. And many people shall say, Come ye, and let us go up to the mountain of the LORD, to the house of the God of Jacob; and he will teach us of his ways,...". **(Isaiah 2v2-3; Micah 4v1-2)***

As the Church allows herself to be all that which God has called Her to be, she will reach that place of being the mountain of the LORD that is established in the top of the mountains. She will reach that place of being exalted above the hills. This will cause the nations to have no choice but to flow to the Church to seek the counsel of God. This is because, currently all the systems of the world are failing and unsustainable. All that will be sustainable will be that which comes from God Almighty.

Make the Watch Strong

Making the watch strong and setting the watchmen is referring to strengthening the prophetic ministry. One of the things that we need to do in gearing for a hostile takeover is to strengthen the prophetic ministry. We need to deepen the Church's understanding of the ministry of prophets. We need to bring the entire Body of Christ to a place and level wherein each believer fully embraces the ministry of prophets.

Over and above that, we also need to ensure that all believers walk in the prophetic. They may not necessarily be prophets but they need to be able to prophesy the Word of the LORD just like the daughters of Philipp the evangelist who prophesied but where not prophets. They operated in the level of the gift of prophecy. Others will operate in the level of the spirit of prophecy just like Saul that prophesied because he was exposed to a prophetically charged up atmosphere.

Strengthening the prophetic ministry is important because, this ministry will help us to navigate the treacherous realms as we engage in spiritual warfare with the enemy. The ministry of the prophet consists of very important gifts of the Holy Spirit. It consists of the gift of word of knowledge, gift of word of wisdom, gift of discernment of spirits and the gift of prophecy.

The first three fall under what is summed up as revelation gifts. It is precisely because of this reason that we need to develop the prophetic ministry in the Church. It is this prophetic ministry that will shine the light of the Word of God and expose the devil's evil schemes. Once the devil's schemes are exposed, it is only then that they can be dealt with effectively.

Prepare Ambushes

This breed of the army of God are a strategic people. They are not driven merely by their emotion and zeal. They are strategic in their approach to the enemy. When they are approaching their target, they are calculative. They know exactly how to position themselves in such a manner that they are not detected by their targets. They are able to "fly under the radar". With this army of God, there will be no media noise surrounding their takeovers. Most will learn of their accomplishments long after they are done and dusted.

In closing, it is very critical for every child of God to understand and fully embrace the need to gear up for a hostile takeover. As alluded to above, this gearing up entails preparation. It is preparation for warfare and spiritual battle. It would be irresponsible of any believer to engage in spiritual warfare and battle without the necessary preparation.

Chapter Fifteen

Exposing Babylon

Throughout this book, we have made reference to Babylon without giving much detail about it. As you will have noted and as indicated in the "Introduction" part of this book, the message of this book is based on the Biblical law called; *"the law of double reference* or *the law of double fulfilment of prophecy"*. With that understanding in mind, we will now take a look at certain traits and attributes of Babylon so we can uncover modern day Babylon. For the purposes of this book, we will not take an exhaustive approach but will make use of a few such traits and attributes of Babylon.

Ancient Babylon

At this point we will firstly look at a few attributes, traits and characteristics of Ancient Babylon. Once we are done with that, we will look at how those attributes, traits and characteristics of Ancient Babylon; are reflected, alive and dominant in Modern Day Babylon.

1. **Cruel and Violent**

   *"I am raising up the Babylonians, a cruel and violent people" **(Habakkuk 1:6 NLT).***

The background to this verse is a state of lawlessness and sinfulness in the nation of Israel. It is a state wherein the wicked outnumbered the just. Corruption, sin and lawlessness reigned supreme in the nation of Israel to an extent that even their judiciary was compromised. Their courts judged in favour of the rich and the poor were literally a prey. At this stage, the nation of Israel was characterised by violence hence Habakkuk cried for the intervention of God. The above verse is how God responded to Habakkuk and told him that He was raising the Babylonians to judge Israel.

One of the ways in which God describes the Babylonians is that they are cruel and violent. The word *"cruel"* means *"wilfully causing pain or suffering to others, or feeling no concern about it"*. The other dictionary defines the word *"cruel"* as *"extremely unkind and unpleasant and causing pain to people or animals intentionally"*. Some of the synonyms of the word *"cruel"* are *"brutal"*, *"savage"*, *"inhuman"*, *barbaric"*, *"brutish"*, *"bloodthirsty"*, *"vicious"* and many others.

Babylonians were not just cruel but were also violent. The word *"violent"* means *"using or involving physical force intended to hurt, damage, or kill someone or something"*. The Merriam-Webster dictionary defines the word *"violent"* as *"marked by the use of usually harmful or destructive physical force"*. The synonyms of the word *"violent"* include the words *"intense"*, *"extreme"*, *"strong"*, *"powerful"*, *"forceful"*, *"wild"*, *"turbulent"*, *"tempestuous"*, *"intemperate"*, *"unrestrained"*, *"ungovernable"*, *"unmanageable"*, *"inordinate"*, *"immoderate"*, *"excessive"* and many others.

The above two words are some of the descriptive words that God uses when He describes Babylon. Historic Biblical Babylon was notorious for being cruel. They intentionally inflicted or caused pain on others. The default disposition of Babylon is that it enjoyed seeing people in suffering, pain and misery. That is what amused the ancient Babylonians. They were a bloodthirsty people and kingdom.

Babylon was also a violent kingdom. They only employed violence and force to get what they wanted. Their use of force was normally intended to; hurt, damage or even kill someone or something. Going as far as killing someone was not an issue for the Babylonians. The only thing that mattered to them was the achievement of their objective. Babylon had no regard whatsoever for the life of both humans and animals. If that particular life was an impediment to their objective, it was expendable.

Just like Ancient Babylon, our world is currently characterised by violence and cruelty. This violence and cruelty occurs in virtually every level. There is cruelty and violence among; nations, racial groups, tribes, colleagues, families and many other sectors of society. In the level of nations, there are nations that manipulate other nations for their own benefit. The stronger nations deliberately mislead the other nations with the sole intention of controlling the resources of the weaker nations.

This is particularly very prevalent between Africa and the West, some pockets of Asia with China in particular and Europe. The policies and so called 'partnerships' entered into between Africa (and other so called third world countries) and the West (and most recently the East) are rooted in cruelty and always result in the deliberate introduction of misery, suffering and pain for the majority of Africans.

In places wherein the West is unable to get its way, they simply employ violent means. This can be by either going directly into war with the nation concerned, just like the USA did in Iraq on two occasions for the control of the oil. Iraq was demonised through the media so that the nefarious and evil agenda could be legitimized. This resulted in the toppling of the properly instituted government of Iraq. The same thing happened in Libya.

If the West does not engage in direct warfare and confrontation with the nation whose natural resources they are targeting, then they finance instability through the funding of rebel groups. The said rebel groups are financed and armed by those intending to illegally exploit the natural resources of such a nation. It is normal for rebel groups to control strategic areas with natural resources. Those that are funding them are given access to mine these areas and make billions of dollars out of the resources illegally mined or extracted from rebel controlled areas.

There is a worldly saying that goes like; *"money makes the world go round"*. In the United States of America they have an informal way of referring to their currency. They call it the *"almighty dollar"*. It is this deep rooted love of money that causes our society to be very cruel and violent. It is because Babylon teaches us that without money we are worthless, hence people end up become both cruel and violent to get money.

All of the above is the work of the king of Babylon. The king of Babylon is the reigning principality that influences and manipulates the hearts and minds of the people of the world to behave in this manner. The king of Babylon is the prince of this world that Jesus Christ mentioned in John 14 and verse 30. Remember the words of Jesus Christ when He says; *"The thief cometh not, but for to steal, and to kill, and to destroy:..." (John 10:10).*

2. Terrible and Dreadful

"They are terrible and dreadful: their judgment...."
(Habakkuk 1:7).

The dictionary meaning of the word *"terrible"* is *"extremely bad"* or *"notably unattractive or objectionable [behaviour]"*, or *"strongly repulsive"*. Terrible is one of the words that God uses to describe Babylonians. They were a terrible people. They were extremely bad and their behaviour was highly objectionable. The Babylonians did not ascribe to moral standards and goodly behaviour. Theirs was always the opposite of all that which is just, good, true and right. This is what made them extremely bad.

Babylon is not only terrible, it is also dreadful. The dictionary definition of the word *"dreadful"* is *"causing or involving great suffering, fear, or unhappiness, extremely bad or serious"*. Some of the synonyms of the word *"dreadful"* include *"frightful"*, *"horrible"*, *"grim"*, *"dire"*, *"awful"*, *"horrifying"*, *"gruesome"*, *"horrendous"*, *"tragic"*, *"calamitous"* and many others. This was the nature of Babylon. Babylon causes great suffering, fear and unhappiness. It glories in causing calamity, tragedy and horror.

Today's world is just as terrible and dreadful as Ancient Babylon. We have already learned that the word *"terrible"* means *"extremely bad" or "notably unattractive or objectionable [behaviour]", or "strongly repulsive"*. This is the current state of the broader society. It is a state of extremely bad, notably unattractive and objectionable behaviour. There is a very obvious and notable progressive decline in the moral standards of society. It even goes as far as being acceptable and promoted.

This is a departure from all that which is good, right, just and true. This is the state that Jesus Christ speaks about when he says; *"And this is the condemnation, that light is come into the world, and men loved darkness rather than light, because their deeds were evil. For every one that doeth evil hateth the light, neither cometh to the light, lest his deeds should be reproved"* **(John 3:19-20).**

One needs not look far to see the terrible state of our society. Just a mere scroll into social media, television and listening to radio will reveal so much bad, notably unattractive and objectionable behaviour. What makes matters worse is that this terrible state of affairs is being celebrated. This is made very clear by the number of followers some lewd social media pages have.

On top of that, our society is dreadful. As we have already indicated before, the word *"dreadful"* means *"causing or involving great suffering, fear, or unhappiness, extremely bad or serious"*. It is so unfortunate that most of this bad, notably unattractive and objectionable behaviour often result in unhappy endings. It mostly results in great suffering.

One of the most notable results of this bad, notably unattractive and objectionable behaviour is contracting of HIV/AIDS. This results in people suffering in silence and far away from the crowd that embraced their objectionable and lewd behaviour. The other result that is common is many road fatalities as a result of drunken driving. It is irresponsible to get behind the wheel of a vehicle when one is drunk and results, in many instances, not only in the death of the culprit but also many innocent people.

Once again, this is the work of the king of Babylon.

3. Babylonians are a Law to Themselves

"……; they are a law to themselves…" ***(Habakkuk 1:7 NIV)***.

Babylonians were a law to themselves. They were a rebellious people that listened only to and acted according to their desires. They had no sense of accountability none whatsoever. They had no regard nor honour or reverence for Almighty God. They simply walked in their own ways and did whatever that they wanted to do. Actually Babylon was ungovernable.

In the book of Genesis 11, we find the Babylonians being really a law unto themselves. This they did when they departed from the principles of God. You make be asking the question; "how did they do that?" If you remember, the account of Genesis 11 is the story of the founding of Babylon wherein they built themselves a tower that would reach unto heaven. The Bible says;

> *"And the whole earth was of one language, and of one speech. And it came to pass, as they journeyed from the east, that they found a plain in the land of* **Shinar**; *and they dwelt there. And they said one to another, Go to, let us make brick, and burn them thoroughly. And they had brick for stone, and slime had they for morter"* **(Genesis 11:1-3).**

Stone and bricks are building blocks and therefore stand symbolic of life governing and life building principles. The Babylonians forsook the naturally occurring stone and mortar and replaced them with brick and slime. The difference between the stone and mortar, and brick and slime, is that stone and mortar represent the principles of the Word of God whilst brick and slime represent manmade ideas and concepts.

In fact The Message translation says; *"A dreadful and terrible people, making up its own rules as it goes"*. This is the foundation of Babylon and what makes Babylon to stray further and further away from God and therefore more and more of a law to themselves.

We are living in a time of growing lawlessness. Because mankind has rebelled against God and came out from under the rule and authority of God, society is now led by the king of Babylon. The larger segment of society is under the leadership, control and manipulation of the king of Babylon even though their majority is not aware.

Remember the Bible says; *"Whoever digs a pit may fall into it; whoever breaks through a wall may be bitten by a snake"* ***(Ecclesiastes 10:8 NIV).*** This rebellion against God is what has given room to the king of Babylon. When mankind rejects the Word of God, they unintentionally break the wall of God's protection around their lives. This opens room for the serpent to bite and devour.

What most people do not realize is that, the king of Babylon, satan or the devil does not ask for your permission in order to come into your life. The only thing that he looks for is an opening. He looks for an opportunity to come in. Remember that he is a thief and just like a thief in the natural will look for a weak spot in your property before breaking in, so does the devil in your life.

The sad reality is that this happens not only with individuals but with families and nations. Nations reject the Word of God by enacting legislation that is diametrically opposed to the principles of the Word of God. In this way, a nation is making its own building blocks and/or principles. That is what eventually leads nations astray. It is the biting of the serpent, the king of Babylon. That is why the Bible says; *"Blessed is the nation whose God is the LORD"* ***(Psalm 33:12).***

4. Babylon Promotes Its Own Honour

"......; they are a law to themselves and promote their own honour" **(Habakkuk 1:7 NIV).**

Self-promotion and self-exaltation was one of the key descriptive of Babylon. This need for self-promotion, self-exaltation and self-aggrandisement comes from Babylon's sense of self importance and pride. There is a lot of scriptural evidence in the Bible that gives us a very vivid picture into how Babylon viewed itself. These scriptures expose the sense of self-importance and self-promotion that Babylon had about it. Some of the scriptures read as follow;

"<u>And thou saidst, I shall be a lady forever:</u> so that thou didst not lay these things to thy heart, neither didst remember the latter end of it. Therefore hear now this, thou that art given to pleasures, that dwellest carelessly, <u>that sayest in thine heart, I am, and none else beside me; I shall not sit as a widow, neither shall I know the loss of children</u>" **(Isaiah 47:7-8).**

The above scripture, especially the underlined parts, give us a very clear picture of the level of self-promotion and self-importance that was the driving force in the heart of Babylon. It is in this state of drunken intoxication with self-exaltation that Babylon even goes as far as saying; *"I am forever-the eternal queen! (NIV).*

She even goes further and says; *"I am, and there is none besides me" (NIV).* As the intention was in building the tower of Babel, Jeremiah prophesied that; *"Though Babylon should mount up to heaven, and though she should fortify the height of her strength, yet from me shall spoilers come unto her, saith the LORD" **(Jeremiah 51:53).***

It is very clear from the above scripture that a big part of the mission of Babylon is to keep climbing. Babylon is such a climber to an extent that God says even if She (Babylon) should mount up to heaven She will be brought down from there. This reveals to us the heart of the king of Babylon, Lucifer that became satan. The Bible tells us the following;

> *"How art thou fallen from heaven, O Lucifer, son of the morning! How art thou cut down to the ground, which didst weaken the nations! For thou hast said in thine heart, I will ascend into heaven, I will exalt my throne above the stars of God: I will sit also upon the mount of the congregation, in the sides of the north: I will ascend above the heights of the clouds; I will be like the most High" **(Isaiah 14:12-14).***

This self-promotion, self-exaltation and self-aggrandising is the compelling spirit of Babylon. It compels the inhabitants of Babylon to an extent that they even go as far as competing with God. This is a spirit of deception that deceives the inhabitants of Babylon. The source of this spirit of deception and delusion is non-other than satan himself.

In this regard our society is not different from Ancient Babylon. We live in an age of vanity and promotion of self. It is the days of social climbing. There is even a saying about *climbing the corporate ladder.* Most of the time people that are focused of achieving significance, status, fame and popularity do so by fleshly means.

That is why what matters to them is the objective of attaining status, fame, significance, popularity, materials and riches. Because it is only their objective that matters to them, they end up not caring one bit about how they attain those things. Others will backstab and even betray colleagues, friends and even family to attain the objective. Others even go as far as to sleep their way to the top. The said reality is that it is no longer just women who sleep their way to the top, even men do it.

This is all done in the effort of promoting oneself. These people do not pay attention to the Word of God that tells us that; *"....promotion cometh neither from the east, nor from the west, nor from the south. But God is the judge: he putteth down one, and setteth up another"* **(Psalms 75:6-7).** All this striving and self-promotion is in an effort to attain perishable things that have no eternal significance. These perishable things are also pursued for selfish reasons with no plan to positively impact other people's lives.

5. Babylon Despises Authority

"They mock kings and scoff at rulers" **(Habakkuk 1:10).**

Because of the sense of superiority that Babylon and Babylonians have over everybody else, they end up mocking and despising any other legitimately established authority.

Babylonians only honour and revere their own king. It is easy to understand why they only honour their own king. It is because their king, satan, is the king of pride.

Because the inhabitants of Babylon are the subjects and servants of the king of Babylon, they are next in line. This is the line of pride and self- importance. Anyone who is not a subject or a servant of the king of pride is looked down upon with disdain by both, the king of Babylon and his servants and/or subjects.

As we have seen with ancient Babylon, the king of Babylon alongside the inhabitants of Babylon despise all forms of authority. This is just like the Babylonians despised everyone else that was not a Babylonian, so do people of modern day Babylon. This is the sense of pride and a superiority complex even towards properly constituted authority that does not belong in the camp of the Babylonians.

In our day and age, this type of pride and disregard for authority manifests itself in various ways. Among the ways in which it manifests itself are; racial pride, national pride, financial pride and many other ways. Racial pride sees people who consider themselves as superior race to others looking down on and despising the authorities of other racial groups that they consider inferior to themselves.

National pride is also no different. Most people from the so called super powers or wealthy nations have an arrogant attitude towards authorities of the nations they consider inferior to their own nation. This manifests itself in simple things like visa applications wherein most expect special treatment because they are from a so called super power.

This attitude is also prevalent among those who are being solicited as potential investors. Some of them show their disdain for the authorities from so called poor nations by setting ridiculous demands before they can come and invest their money. Such ridiculous demands see these so called investors coming into the so called inferior countries not as partners in building and developing that nation but as employers that take the largest chunk of the profits and consign everybody to employment. They are normally able to pack up and leave at a moment's notice and leave scores of people unemployed and families destitute without being held accountable.

6. Babylon's Strength is its god

> *"But they are deeply guilty, for their own strength is their god"* ***(Habakkuk 1:11).***

In the Bible, Babylon is described on many occasions as a very strong and mighty nation. It is this level of strength and might that made Babylon to be such a dominant kingdom in the earth. There is plenty of historical and Biblical evidence about the dominance and extent of the kingdom of Babylon. In the book of Daniel, King Nebuchadnezzar had a dream. The dream that he saw, among other things, also revealed the level and extent of the Babylonian kingdom in the earth.

In reality, there are two dreams that King Nebuchadnezzar had. Both of these dreams revealed the extent of the dominance of the Babylonian kingdom. In the first dream, Nebuchadnezzar saw a huge statue with a gold head, arms and breasts of silver, belly and thighs of brass, legs of iron and feet partly iron and partly clay. Part of Daniel's interpretation of that dream reads as follows;

> *"Thou, O king, art a king of kings: for the God of heaven hath given thee a kingdom, power, and strength, and glory. And wheresoever the children of men dwell, the beast of the field and the fowls of the heaven hath he given to thine hand, and hath made thee ruler over them all. Thou art this head of gold"* ***(Daniel 2:37-78).***

In the second dream that King Nebuchadnezzar had, he saw a tree in the middle of the earth. The height of the tree was great. The tree grew, and was strong, and the height of the tree reached unto heaven, and it was visible to the ends of the earth. Again part of Daniel's interpretation of this second dream that King Nebuchadnezzar had reads as follows;

> *"The tree that thou sawest, which grew, and was strong, whose height reached unto the heaven, and the sight thereof to all the earth; Whose leaves were fair, and the fruit thereof much, and in it was meat for all; under which the beasts of the field dwelt, and upon whose branches the fowls of the heaven had their habitation: It is thou, O king, that art grown and become strong: for thy greatness is grown, and*

reacheth unto heaven, and thy dominion to the end of the earth" ***(Daniel 4:20-22).***

The above two scripture quotations give us a very vivid picture of the dominance of the Babylonian Empire. It is this level of dominance that led to the deception of Babylon thinking that it is their own strength that gave them such power and dominance. This arrogance and worship of one's strength by Babylon can be clearly seen and heard in the life and words of King Nebuchadnezzar when he said;

"The king spake, and said, Is not this great Babylon, that I have built for the house of the kingdom by the might of my power, and for the honour of my majesty?" ***(Daniel 4:30).***

King Nebuchadnezzar attributed the achievement of the greatness and dominance of Babylon to his own power and strength. This is despite the fact that Daniel had on two occasions told him that *the God of heaven hath given thee a kingdom, power, and strength, and glory"* ***(Daniel 2:37).*** This is a perfect demonstration of how Babylon worships its own strength. They take credit for that which is given to them by God and that is one of their biggest sins. This attitude and disposition causes them to commit idolatry and therefore end up not seeing a need for God in their lives. In their own eyes, they are self-sufficient.

One of the main characteristics, attributes and traits of Modern Day Babylon is that it is, just like ancient Babylon, characterised by its strength and dominance. These are a people that have both amazing levels of intellectual and physical strength. They have harnessed and developed their intellectual strength by much studying.

As it should, this intellectual and academic strength has resulted in many technological, financial and industrial advancements. There have been many notable advancements in the fields of engineering, communication, medical science, and many other fields of study. Others even attempted to find God by means of research and development the financing of which ranges in billions of dollars. When they did not find God by carnal (research and development) means, they erroneously concluded that "there is no God".

They have also harnessed and developed their physical strength by means of developing very advanced military artillery. All of this, they have achieved by means of research and development. As a result of this wonderful research and development, they even managed to develop weapons of mass destruction and intercontinental heat seeking ballistic missiles. Because of this level of super physical strength, they once again concluded that there is no power greater than their own weapons.

As a result of this, modern day Babylon is characterised by the magnifying and worshipping of one's intellectual and physical strength and abilities. This is the sin that modern day Babylon, much like ancient Babylon, is guilty of. Today people are encouraged to believe in themselves without acknowledging the intellectual and physical strength that they possess actually comes from Almighty God.

I do not want to leave you with the impression that I have something against intellectual and physical strength or even research and development. On the contrary, I think all believers should embrace intellectual and physical strength, as long as they know that they have received such from God and give the honour and glory to God for it.

Morden Day Babylon

One does not need to be a rocket scientist to notice that the above characteristics, traits and attributes are prevalent in today's society. These are prevalent in virtually every single sector of society from government, business and economics, education, church, entertainment and all other sectors of society.

In conclusion, these are just a few of the traits and characteristics that are prevalent in our world today. These very attributes, traits and characteristics are the very things that keep people from worshipping and honouring God. This is the goal and objective of the king of Babylon. It is to cause an irreparable chasm between mankind and Almighty God.

Chapter Sixteen

The Fall of Babylon

It must have been in either 1999 or the year 2000 when I read an article in the Believers Voice of Victory magazine. The article was written by Kenneth Copeland. I don't really remember the title of the article but I will try to paraphrase the part that stuck with me. In the article Kenneth Copeland said;

"Every ten to fifteen years there are either rumours of wars or wars breaking out. When this happens, it is normally accompanied by the release of a new move of God. God works in cycles and the devil also works in cycles. The difference between these cycles is that God works in life cycles whilst the devil works in death cycles. That is why Jesus Christ says; "The thief comes not, but for to steal, and to kill, and to destroy: I am come that they might have life and that they might have it more abundantly.

The devil understands the life cycles of God but he cannot do anything to stop them. The best that the devil will do is to unleash a death cycle in anticipation of the life cycle of God so as to blind the Church from perceiving and receiving the life cycle that God is releasing" **(Paraphrase).**

Now, with that kind of background and understanding, I want to submit to you that God released a life cycle in the year 2001 and the devil also released a death cycle so as to blind the Church from perceiving and receiving the life cycle that

God was releasing. Thankfully, the Bible teaches us that; *"Surely the Lord GOD will do nothing, but he revealeth his secret unto his servants the prophets" (**Amos 3:7**).* The Bible also teaches us that apostles and prophets are stewards of the mysteries of God **(1 Corinthians 4:1)**.

It was in the month of August year 2000 when God started talking to me about the Cyrus Anointing. Something very interesting happened to me in a space of about a year since God started talking to me about the Cyrus Anointing. It must have been from around the 21st August 2001 until the 10th of September 2001. I would be sleeping and hear the voice of the LORD over and over saying; *"I have pronounced judgment upon Babylon, I have pronounced judgment upon Babylon, I have pronounced judgment upon Babylon".*

I kept hearing the voice of the LORD saying the same thing over and over every single day and night when I laid down. Sometimes I would be half asleep and still hear the LORD saying the same thing. As most people will know on the 11th of September 2001, two hijacked aircrafts (packed to capacity) were deliberately crashed into the twin towers of the World Trade Centre. This resulted in the very tragic collapse of the twin towers and the death of many innocent people.

A lot of people and families lost their loved ones. It was a very tragic and dreadful thing to watch on the television. It took the nation of America many years to heal from that terrible, senseless attack and mass murder of innocent people. These were people that were working hard for their families and their loved ones. So diabolic and coordinated was the 9/11 attack so much that another hijacked aircraft was deliberately crashed into the Pentagon, the military command centre of the USA. Thanks to the bravery of the American passengers and who were in another hijacked flight. Their bravery saw them choosing to self-sacrifice by crashing the aircraft and thereby ensuring that it never reached its intended target.

Now, I submit to you that the 9/11 terror attack against the nation of America was a death cycle that satan unleashed so as to blind the eyes of the Church from the life cycle (God's pronounced judgment upon Babylon) that Almighty God was and is still releasing. The interesting thing about the enemy is that, he has a tendency of playing right into the plan of God. I suppose that is the exact reason why the Bible says; *"You intended to harm me, but God intended it all for good"* ***(Genesis 50:20 NLT).*** The devil meant to cause harm with the 9/11 attack and he did inflict very serious sorrow and pain. In the greater scheme of things though, the enemy played into the plan of God.

You may be asking; "what do I mean by that". Let me clarify. The 9/11 terrorists could have chosen any nation, any city and any building in the Western World but somehow they chose the nation of the United States of America. Not only that, but they also chose New York, Manhattan and the twin towers that housed the World Trade Centre.

If you look very closes at the Babylon described in the Bible, you will notice that there are prophetic parallels between Manhattan and ancient Babylon. At this point I want to look at and unpack a few of these prophetic parallels between the 9/11 attack and the Babylon that is so clearly described and defined in the Bible. There are a lot of these prophetic parallels but for the purpose of our study, we will take only three and also clarify that Babylon has already been judged and has started falling.

Tower of Babel and the Twin Towers

The first prophetic parallel that we will look at is between the Tower of Babel and the Twin Towers of the World Trade Centre. The founding of Babylon is mentioned in the book of Genesis chapter eleven when mankind was united with the purpose of building a tower that would reach unto heaven. The Bible tells us that;

> "And it came to pass, as they journeyed from the east, that they found a plain in the land of Shinar; <u>and they dwelt there</u>. And they said one to another, Go to, <u>let us make brick,</u> and burn them thoroughly. <u>And had brick for stone, and slime had they for mortar</u>. And they said, Go to, <u>let us build us a city and a tower, whose top may reach unto heaven; and let us make us a name, lest we be scattered abroad upon the face of the whole earth</u>" ***(Genesis 11:2-4).***

From a physical standpoint and perspective, the tower of Babel is comparative to the twin towers. In the previous chapter we have alluded to part of the above scripture. At this point we will touch on most of the above scripture. One of the first things that we notice in the above scripture is that, as they journeyed from the east they found a plain in the land of Shinar (Babylonia).

A plain is level ground. From a construction and engineering point of view this tends to be the easiest land to build on. The Bible tells us that *they dwelt there*. They chose to settle in the area that seemed to be a comfort zone. It was a place that did not require much effort. They did not just settle there, they also came up with their own principles of life and living. Instead of the naturally occurring substances (stone and mortar made by God), they made their own (brick and slime) artificial man-made principles and rules.

On top of all of that, they went on and conspired to build themselves a city and a tower whose top would reach unto heaven. By doing this, the Babylonians really showed that they were not a people of faith. They were impatient and could not wait for God to direct their course. In fact they did not even acknowledge, believe in or obey God. They truly were independent of God.

If we look at Manhattan New York today, from various imagery on the internet Manhattan appears to be fairly plain and level. Its topography appears to be fairly level and consistent. This matches the plain that was found by man in the book of Genesis chapter eleven.

Secondly the Bible tells us that when they found the plain, they decided to settle and dwell there. Not only that but they decided to build themselves a city and a tower that would reach to heaven. In chapter twelve of the book of Genesis, the Bible tells us that God called Abram out of Ur of the Chaldees and told him to go into a land that God would show him. The book of Hebrews chapter eleven tells us that;

> *"By faith Abraham, when he was called to go out into a place which he should after receive for an inheritance, obeyed; and he went out, not knowing whither he went. By faith he sojourned in the land of promise, as in a strange country, dwelling in tabernacles with Isaac and Jacob, the heirs with him of the promise: For he looked for a city which hath foundations, whose builder and maker is God"* **(Hebrews 11:8-10).**

A city has life and livelihood. There are families, businesses, worship, entertainment, media, academic institutions, commerce, administration and governance in a city. These are just a few of the constituent elements that make up a city. It goes without mentioning that there is headship and authority in a city. In the case of Abraham in the above scripture, he walked by faith.

Abraham did not just decide to settle anywhere. He was patient and obedient to Almighty God. The Bible records that he dwelt in tabernacles for as long as he was still on the journey. This points us to the willingness of Abraham to adjust and adapt as he journeyed along. This adjusting and adaptation would be in obedience to God. As a result, Abraham did not build himself a permanent fixed structure or city. He continued to search for a city which had foundations that were built and made by Almighty God. The journey of the Babylonians on the other hand is in stark contrast to the journey of Abraham.

It is evident that the journey of the Babylonians was in stark contrast to the journey of Abraham. If it had not been, then

God would not have seen the need to come down and confuse their languages. The reason why God had to confuse their languages was because what the Babylonians were beginning to do went against one of the most fundamental commands that God gave to mankind.

That command is the command to *"Be fruitful, and multiply, and replenish the earth, and subdue it: and have dominion over the fish of the sea, and over the fowl of the air, and over every living thing that moveth upon the earth"* **(Genesis 1:28).** Effectively, the declaration of the Babylonians contradicted the command of God to *"replenish the earth, and subdue it"*. The Babylonians went and established themselves in a permanently fixed city that came as a result of their own conception. That city did not come as a result of an instruction from God.

The Babylonians decided to build a city and a tower for themselves. The Bible tells us they decided to settle in the plain of Shinar that they found. In relation to Manhattan and the twin towers this obviously directs us to the glaring physical prophetic parallel of the tower of Babel and the twin towers that crashed on that tragic 9/11 terror attack, the death cycle of the devil.

Even further than merely the physical prophetic parallel of the towers, this also directs us further to the financial and economic establishment of Manhattan. According to Wikipedia; *"Manhattan is often described as the cultural, financial, media and entertainment capital of the world"*. As the cultural, financial, media and entertainment capital of the world, Manhattan and New York, by extension, can be regarded as the originator of all the financial, cultural, media and entertainment polies and principles of the world. It is a well-known, undeniable and widely accepted fact that one of the things that the United States of America has been able to successfully export to all the nations of the earth is its culture. This is evidenced in many things including music, movies, sports, clothing and many others. All the other nations of the world take their cue from Manhattan New York and the USA with regards to financial, cultural, media and entertainment concepts.

This culture that the USA has successfully exported is; over and above excellence in music, television and movies, clothing, finance, media; a culture of moral decadence. In other words, Manhattan New York, in fact the entire USA, is the world leader in all sectors of society. The world over has fully adopted and embraced the brick and slime principles of Manhattan New York. All the cultural, financial, media and entertainment trends of the world are set by Manhattan New York, USA. This is just like what the Bible says about Babylon. Remember the Bible teaches us that;

> *"For all nations have drunk of the wine of the wrath of her fornication, and the kings of the earth have committed fornication with her and the merchants of the earth are waxed rich through the abundance of her delicacies"* ***(Revelations 18:3).***

In the same manner that Babylon caused all the nations to drink of the wine of the wrath of her fornication and caused kings of the earth to commit fornication with her; so did Manhattan New York influence the culture, finance, media, entertainment and all other sectors of the nations of the world. In other words Babylon developed their own principles (brick and slime) and corrupted and contaminated the nations with their brick and slime that promotes departure from God.

As already mentioned above, Babylon departed from the principles and ways of God when they, unlike Abraham, decided to settle and founded their own city that was built with their own man-made principles and ideas. Because of embracing the influence and principles of Manhattan New York, the nations of the earth were also led astray and they departed from God.

This is also the complexion of the Church that settles and does not embrace the Great Commission to go into the entire world and make disciples of nations. They look inward and are selfish. They are merely concerned about building their own tower and making a name for themselves. This type of a Church is only concerned about artificial and cosmetic things such as having the most beautiful or biggest buildings and receiving the most offering. They are concerned about television or radio ministries. Please note that I am not suggesting that there is anything wrong with having big, beautiful buildings or being on television or radio. I am simply pointing out that the Babylonian Church is a Church whose primary concern is those things.

The construction and founding of Babylon as founded in Genesis chapter eleven was meant solely for the benefit of the people of Babylon. It is because of the fact that Babylon was founded solely for the benefit of the people of Babylon that their principles and policies (brick and slime) were biased towards them. This is the reality of our time even today. The financial and economic policies crafted in the financial and economic capital of the world, Manhattan New York in the USA, are biased and skewed in favour of the USA. The objective of making such policies is so that they can make a name for themselves and remain ahead and on top of everyone else.

We have seen this with ancient Biblical Babylon. It was after king Nebuchadnezzar defeated and conquered Judah and Israel that he took the best of the best, the cream of the crop from Israel and Judah and took them to slavery in Babylon. He only left the poorest sort of people in Israel and Judah so that they could till the ground and send the best of the produce to Babylon. Daniel, Hananiah (Shadrack), Mishael (Meshach), and Azariah (Abednego) are a typical example of the cream of the crop that were taken from Judah and Israel and sent to Babylon for the benefit of Babylon. It is revealed in the Bible that; Daniel, Hananiah, Mishael and Azariah were of royal descent and they were found to be ten times better (in terms of competence) than all the wise men of Babylon. It is a well-known fact that slavery benefitted the West immensely.

As mentioned before, the king of Babylon left only the poorest sort of the people in the land of Judah and Israel to work the land and send the best produce of the land to Babylon. That trend continues even to today. The nations of the world are still producing and exporting A grade produce to the nations of the West. This is to ensure that the West is kept ahead of everyone else both in terms of physical health and strength as well as their economy and financial strength. That is why the Bible teaches us that the kings of the earth have committed fornication with her and the merchants of the world, that export the best produce to her, wax rich because of her delicacies.

Just like the tower of Babel was a symbol of pride, self-importance and self-exaltation for ancient Babylon, so did the twin towers mark the skyline of the USA as a symbol of pride for the USA. It was a symbol of self-exaltation just like ancient Babylon said;

> *"And thou saidst, I shall be a lady for ever: so that thou didst not lay these things to thy heart, neither didst remember the latter end of it. Therefore hear now this, thou that art given to pleasures, that dwellest carelessly, that sayest in thine heart, I am, and none else beside me; I shall not sit as a widow, neither shall I know the loss of children:"* **(Isaiah 47:7-8).**

There is that self-exaltation, sense of self-importance and pride in the words uttered by Babylon. The twin towers of the World Trade Centre were said to be the tallest buildings in the world until such a time that a taller building than them was constructed in Chicago. Obviously that has been outdone and dwarfed by new skyscrapers that have been developed in Dubai in the United Arab Emirates.

Manhattan Island and Babylon Sits on Water

"O thou that dwellest upon many waters, abundant in treasures, thine end is come, and the measure of thy covetousness" ***(Jeremiah 51:13).***

"....Come hither; I will shew unto thee the judgment of the great whore that sitteth upon many waters" ***(Revelations 17:1).***

It is made very clear in the Bible that Babylon sits on many waters. According to the Pulpit Commentary of the Bible, the "many waters" mentioned in Jeremiah above are in reference to the Euphrates River as well as the canals, dykes and marshes which surrounded ancient Babylon. Manhattan also sits on water. It is bounded by three rivers namely; Hudson River, Harlem River and the East River. This is the most obvious physical prophetic parallel between Ancient Babylon and Manhattan. This is obviously from the physical perspective and stand point.

In the book of Revelations we get an understanding of the true meaning and significance of the "many waters". The angel that spoke to John told him the mystery of the beast that sat upon many waters and said that; *"....., The waters which thou sawest, where the whore sitteth, are peoples, and multitudes, and nations, and tongues"* ***(Revelations 17:15).*** According to Revelations the waters that Babylon sits upon are peoples, multitudes and nations and tongues.

According to Wikipedia Manhattan is *also one of the most densely populated areas in the world, with a census-estimated*

2017 population of 1,664,727 living in a land area of 22.83 square miles (59.13km²), or 72,918 residents per square mile (28,154/km²). On business days, the influx of commuters increases this number to over 3.9 million, or more than 170,000 people per square mile (65,600/km²).

New York is one of, if not the most culturally diverse city in the world. It boasts a very large immigrant population. To others, the city's openness to newcomers makes it the archetype of a "nation of immigrants". According to Wikipedia; *In 2000, 36% of the city's population was foreign-born.* This obviously presents us with a very apparent similarity to ancient Babylon. Babylon subdued and enslaved many other nations than just the Israelites. It is because of that that the racial, cultural and ethnic composition of Babylon was so diverse.

That is exactly why Babylon is said to be sitting upon peoples, multitudes, nations and tongues. Sitting upon peoples, multitudes, nations and tongues conveys the attitude and disposition of Babylon towards these peoples, multitudes, nations and tongues. She sits on the peoples, multitudes, nations and tongues to oppress, manipulate and control them. This is an attitude and posture of dominance that Babylon is exercising upon the peoples, multitudes, nations and tongues.

I wish to remind the reader that the real Babylon that we are warring against is spiritual not a physical city or nation. Hence Babylon represents the demonic entities that are sitting on peoples, multitudes, nations and tongues to oppress, manipulate, control and dominate them. In this regard, New

York is merely a physical prophetic parallel to the ancient city of Babylon as outlined in the Bible.

Babylon and Manhattan New York Are Abundant in Treasures

One of the main characteristics mentioned about Babylon is that it is abundant in treasures. The Bible tells us that;

> "*O thou that dwellest upon many waters, <u>abundant in treasures</u>, thine end is come, and the measure of thy covetousness*" ***(Jeremiah 51:13).***

Babylon grew very rich and wealthy both because of its industriousness as well as it pillaging the other nations that they defeated, subdued and dominated. As a result of that Babylon had an abundance of treasures. It had an abundance of gold, silver, precious stones and all things that were precious. As a matter of fact, the book of revelations tells us that Babylon was clothed in fine linen, purple, and scarlet.

In this respect Manhattan is no different from Babylon. It is also very abundant in treasures. In other words it is a very wealthy city. It is a well-known fact that Manhattan New York boasts two stock exchanges, namely; New York Stock Exchange and the NASDAQ. In 2017, the NYSE was said to be the world's largest exchange by market capitalization of its listed companies at US$21.3 trillion as of June 2017. Its average daily trading value was approximately US$169 billion in 2013. NASDAQ on the other hand is said to be the second biggest exchange in the world with a market capitalization of US$7.8 trillion.

Not only that, the pre 9/11 World Trade Centre housed some of the biggest multinational companies in the world. As a matter of fact the rental per square metre rates in Manhattan is amongst the highest if not the highest in the world. This obviously spills into the property purchasing prices for both the residential and commercial property market.

So abundant were the treasures of Babylon that the Bible tells us that the merchants of the world that traded with Babylon grew very rich. Even to this day, Manhattan New York and the United States of America remains one of the favourite export destinations for most entities that are producing and exporting goods. This is because when dealing with the USA, traders know that they will be paid for their goods and they will be well compensated for their goods. This is in contrast to most traders' response when dealing with Asian countries. Most traders tend to be sceptical when dealing with clients from the Asiatic countries. They do not respond as easily as they do when dealing with clients or buyers from the United States of America.

Alright, now we have dealt with the three prophetic parallels between ancient Babylon and the location against which satan chose to unleash his evil and diabolical death cycle, the United States of America. We will now look at the prophetic scriptures regarding the actual fall of Babylon and also unpack how those scriptures have played out in the 9/11 terror attack and how they are yet to play out. I must also mention upfront that there are already a lot of scriptures about the fall of Babylon but for the purpose of our study we will take a look at three verses. If you need to do more reading on the fall of Babylon, please feel free to study, Isaiah 13, 14, 21 and 47, Jeremiah 50 and 51 and Revelations 17 and 18.

The Whole Earth Was Moved At the Taking of Babylon

"At the noise of the taking of Babylon the earth is moved, and the cry is heard among the nations" (Jeremiah 50:46).

"At the sound of Babylon's conquest the earth will quake; a cry will be heard among the nations" (Jeremiah 50:46 CSB).

One of the indications of the fall of Babylon is its worldwide notability and impact. The event is so notable to an extent that the whole earth is moved and the cry of the inhabitants of Babylon reaches to all the nations of the earth. It is an unsettling event not only for the inhabitants of Babylon but for all the nations of the earth. The reason for this kind of impact and reach of the cry of Babylon is because of the kings of the earth that have committed fornication with Babylon as well as the merchants of the earth that traded with Babylon. It is also because of the brutal and violent nature of the attack that God intends to visit upon Babylon.

Now, in the case of the 9/11 terror attack in America, the impact and notability was also on a worldwide scale. It was instant breaking news all around the world. As a matter of fact, Wikipedia says the following; *"The September 11 attacks of 2001, in addition to being a unique act of terrorism, constituted a media event on a scale not seen since the advent of civilian global satellite links, round- the- clock television news organizations and the instant worldwide reaction and debate made possible by the Internet. As a result, most of the events listed below were known by a large portion of the planet's population as they occurred".*

Things will not be different with the continuing fall of Babylon. As indicated earlier on, God Almighty has already pronounced judgment upon Babylon. It is when that Judgment reaches its fullness that the whole earth will be moved and the resulting cry from the fall and collapse of Babylon will be heard among all the nations of the earth. This will be a very difficult time for those that have built their lives in accordance to the patterns of Babylon. Only those who have built their lives upon the Rock of ages will not be moved by the floods and storms that are to come upon Babylon.

The 9/11 Terror Attack and The Fall of Babylon Happened in One Day

> *"Therefore shall her plagues come in one day, death, and mourning, and famine; and she shall be utterly burned with fire: for strong is the Lord God who judgeth her"* ***(Revelations 18:8).***

The 9/11 terror attack on the twin towers of the world trade centre was a very tragic and diabolical attack. Many innocent lives were lost on that day due to the terror attack. So violent and ugly was the attack it gripped the nation of America in never seen before levels of fear. Most people kept indoors and most did not know if it was over but it only took one day and there are no attacks that happened afterwards.

This is yet another indisputable prophetic parallel between the prophesied fall of Babylon and the 9/11 terror attack. Because of a one day incident, America suffered death, mourning and famine. The death and mourning are very obvious as they were felt immediately by the nation of America. The famine on the other hand was felt years later when the 2008 Financial Crisis happened. It was as a result of the 9/11 attack.

What is evident now with the current fall of Babylon is how the financial and economic systems of the world are failing. There are a number of technologic disruptions that are breaking monopolies and rendering certain systems obsolete. One of such disruptions is the emergence of the blockchain technology. The result of the full extent fall of Babylon will be famine for those who are still holding on to the failing Babylonian systems.

Stripping And Repossession of Babylon's Treasures

> "......:a sword is upon her treasures; and they shall be robbed" *(Jeremiah 50:37).*
>
> "...A sword is against her treasuries, and they will be plundered" *(Jeremiah 50:37 CSB).*

A very violent assault on and plundering of the treasures of Babylon is one of the things that can be expected with the fall of Babylon. We have seen a fulfilment of this in the life of King Cyrus when he overthrew Babylon. As God promised King Cyrus by the mouth of Jeremiah, God delivered the treasures of darkness and hidden riches of secret places into the hand of King Cyrus.

There is scriptural evidence that supports the fact that God did indeed deliver the treasures of darkness into the hand of King Cyrus. Remember, the Bible teaches us that *out of the mouth of two to three witnesses shall a matter be established*. There are at least two scriptures that attest to this reality and they read as follows;

> *"Now in the first year of Cyrus king of Persia, that the word of the LORD spoken by the mouth of Jeremiah might be accomplished, the LORD stirred up the spirit of Cyrus king of Persia, that he made a proclamation throughout all his kingdom, and put it also in writing, saying, Thus saith Cyrus king of Persia, All the kingdoms of the earth hath the LORD God of heaven given me; and he hath charged me to build him an house in Jerusalem, whivh is in Judah. Who is there among you of all his people? The LORD his God be with him, and let him go up"* ***(2 Chronicles 36:22-23).***

> *"Now in the first year of Cyrus king of Persia, that the word of the LORD spoken by the mouth of Jeremiah might be accomplished, the LORD stirred up the spirit of Cyrus king of Persia, that he made a proclamation throughout all his kingdom, and put it also in writing, saying, Thus saith Cyrus king of Persia, All the kingdoms of the earth hath the LORD God of heaven given me; and he hath charged me to build him an house in Jerusalem, whivh is in Judah.*

> *Who is there among you of all his people? The LORD his God be with him, and let him go up to Jerusalem. And whosoever remaineth in any place where he sojourneth, let the men of his place help him with silver, and with gold, and with goods, and with beasts, beside the freewill offering for the house of God that is in Jerusalem........Also king Cyrus brought forth the vessels of the house of the LORD, which Nebuchadnezzar had brought forth out of Jerusalem, and had put them in the house of his gods"* ***(Ezra 1:1-4,7)***.

In the words of King Cyrus himself, God had given him all the kingdoms of the earth. It is a universal fact that those who are victors and conquer in a war receive the spoils. The kingdoms that God gave to King Cyrus were kingdoms with commercial activity and resources kept in reserve. These resources came in the form of gold, silver and other precious things. It is a foregone conclusion that the victor is entitled to the spoils of war.

It was no different when King Cyrus overcame and conquered Babylon. Babylon came with all its treasures and hidden riches. As we had indicated in Chapter Nine these were treasures that different Bible Commentaries indicate were hidden by burying underground. It is possible that some of these treasures were hidden in ancient vaults that were designed specifically for concealing the treasures. The fact that these treasures are treasures of darkness also alludes to the fact that the vaults had no windows and therefore light could not access the vaults.

Now during the 9/11 terror attack there was a definite plundering of the treasures that were stored in secret hidden vaults.

In the 9/11 terror attack, there are a number of notable financial losses to the financial establishment of the world. The most notable of them all was in the insurance industry space. According to Wikipedia; *The September 11 attacks themselves resulted in approximately US$40 billion in Insurance losses, making it one of the largest insured events ever.* This means that those who anticipated an attack of this nature were able to claim from their insurers and were compensated for losses that they suffered in the 9/11 terror attack.

The other notable financial loss that took place during the 9/11 terror attack is the closure of New York Stock Exchange, NASDAQ, New York Mercantile Exchange, London Stock Exchange. All banks and financial institutions on Wall Street and in many cities in the USA were evacuated. Stock Exchanges around the world were also closed down and evacuated for fear of follow up terror attacks. The obvious result of the continued closure of the world stock exchanges was loss of revenue as it meant there was no trading activity happening.

A number of the sectors of the economy were severely affected by the 9/11 terror attacks not only domestically in the USA but on a global scale. The most severely and immediately affected sectors included; insurance, travel and tourism and airlines and aviation. On top of all of this, global stock markets dropped very sharply. As currency trading continued, the United States dollar fell sharply against the Euro, British Pound and the Japanese Yen.

The obvious result of the dip in the prices of shares listed in the global stock exchanges is the depletion of the wealth and resources of those that held such shares. It also resulted in the depletion of the market valuation of the companies that were listed in the global stock exchanges. The same applied to those that held their wealth and resources in the United States dollar currency. The devaluation of the United States dollar drastically reduced their wealth.

As the Bible says, with the fall of Babylon, the treasures of Babylon will be plundered. There will be a strategic positioning that will enable those that are anointed with the Cyrus Anointing to plunder the treasures of Babylon. As they listen to and obey the leading of the Holy Spirit, they will be ushered and led into benefitting from the fall of Babylon. This will manifest itself in various ways including divine instructions and guidance in how and where to invest.

One of the notable disruptions that cannot be ignored is the introduction of crypto currencies and the Blockchain Technology. Bitcoin, other crypto currencies and Blockchain technology pose a very serious threat to the financial and banking system of the world. It is a direct threat to the fractional reserve banking system that enables those from the banking establishment to amass to themselves tons and tons of wealth through transaction processing fees. By replacing the trust element that is required in the banking system, Blockchain technology is effectively transferring wealth from the hands of a few individuals and banking organizations into the hands of the masses. Those masses are the ones that are involved in the mining of Bitcoin and other crypo currency (such as Etherium, and others).

A Complete Abandonment of Babylon's Principles and Policies

> *"And they shall not take of thee a stone for a corner, nor a stone for foundations; but thou shalt be desolate for ever, saith the LORD"* ***(Jeremiah 51:26).***

As mentioned before, a stone represents building blocks and therefore building principles. We have already established that Babylon forsook the principles of God by formulating their own principles and policies. In the fall, collapse and absolute destruction of Babylon none of their building blocks and principles will be retrieved and reused. This is because of the extent of the damage to such building blocks and the fact that they will have been proven beyond doubt to be utterly useless, unsustainable and unreliable.

We have seen this with the fall, collapse and absolute destruction of the twin tower during the September 11 attack. The site of the 9/11 towers was never reconstructed again. Instead a museum and a memorial to the 9/11 terror attack was established. This is an undisputable fact that attests to the fall that God pronounced upon Babylon. It attests to the fact that, the devil did indeed choose New York City as the place upon which to unleash his death cycle.

When God's judgment upon Babylon reaches the fullness of time, it will be to an extent that all worldly ways of living will be shunned and forsaken by most of mankind. Those who are stubborn will find themselves perishing with Babylon.

Leave Babylon

> *"Remove out of the midst of Babylon, and go forth out of the land of the Chaldeans, and be as the he goats before the flocks"* ***(Jeremiah 50:8).***

> *"Flee out of the midst of Babylon, and deliver, every man his soul: be not cut off in her iniquity; for this is the time of the LORD'S vengeance; he will render unto her a recompense"* ***(Jeremiah 51:6).***

> *"My people, go ye out of the midst of her, and deliver ye every man his soul from the fierce anger of the LORD"* ***(Jeremiah 51:45).***

> *"And I heard another voice from heaven, saying, Come out of her, my people, that ye be not partakers of her sins, and that ye receive not of her plagues"* ***(Revelations 18:4).***

There is a heavenly call unto every believer, every single born again child of God to depart from Babylon. It is a heavenly call to forsake the ways of the world and embrace the Way of Faith. The Bible teaches us that the just shall live by faith. It also teaches us that whatsoever is not of faith is sin. In the Body of Christ, sin is broadly defined as "missing the mark". In other words, it is missing the mark of the standard of God. It is a failure to do things the way that the Word of God requires us to do things.

Jesus Christ teaches that anyone that hears His words and does them is a wise man that built his house upon a rock and anyone who hears His words and does not do them is a foolish man. The one that hears and does the words of Jesus Christ is like a man that built his house on a rock whilst the one who does not do the words of Jesus Christ is like a foolish man that built his house upon sand. When the storms and hurricanes come, the house built on a rock remained whilst the house built on sand was swept away.

We depart Babylon by laying not for ourselves treasures on earth where moth and rust corrupt and where thieves break through and steal. We depart Babylon by laying up treasures for ourselves in heaven where neither moth nor rust can corrupt and where thieves cannot break through and steal. This is about being in right alignment with the Word of God in every respect of our lives.

In closing, I wish to state that all of the above is not in any way meant to suggest that the United States of America is Babylon. It is merely meant to highlight that, with the death cycle he unleashed, satan unintentionally ended up illuminating the life cycle of God. This, he did by choosing and targeting a place that bears resemblance to ancient Babylon through the above outlined prophetic parallels.

It is also very important to highlight and mention that God has nothing against the people of America as a people and as a nation. God is against the state of moral decadence and objectionable behaviour that is as a result of demonic entities that have set themselves over the nation of America. It is these evil entities that have caused the majority of American citizens to be oppressed, manipulated and therefore controlled by the king of Babylon.

The reader will do well to recall that our warfare is not against flesh and blood but against principalities, against powers, against the rulers of the darkness of this world and against spiritual wickedness in high places. It is these principalities, powers, rulers and spiritual wickedness that manifest themselves not only in the United States of America but in every other nation in the earth. These are the principalities, powers, rulers and spiritual wickedness that God is against.

As for the people of America and every other nation in the earth, God loves them. He loves not only them but also their different lands. Remember Psalms twenty four and verse one teaches us that; *"The earth is the LORD's, and the fullness thereof; the world, and they that dwell therein"*. That which God requires is for His people to return to Him.

www.ingramcontent.com/pod-product-compliance
Lightning Source LLC
Chambersburg PA
CBHW070656100426
42735CB00039B/2171